The Philosophy of the *Daodejing*

THE PHILOSOPHY OF THE
Daodejing

Hans-Georg Moeller

COLUMBIA UNIVERSITY PRESS   NEW YORK

COLUMBIA UNIVERSITY PRESS

Publishers Since 1893
New York   Chichester, West Sussex

Copyright © 2006 Columbia University Press
All rights reserved

Library of Congress Cataloging-in-Publication Data

Moeller, Hans-Georg, 1964–
　　The philosophy of the Daodejing / Hans-Georg Moeller.
　　　　p. cm.
　　Includes bibliographical references and index.
　　ISBN 0-231-13678-1 (hbk. : alk. paper) —
　　ISBN 978-0-231-13679-2 (pbk. : alk. paper)
　　1. Laozi. Dao de jing.   2. Philosophy, Taoist.   I. Title.

BL1900.L35M64 2006
2299.5'1482—dc22

2005055156

The author and Columbia University Press gratefully acknowledge permission to quote from the following works:

Chuang-Tzu: The Inner Chapters, trans. A. C. Graham (Indianapolis, Ind.: Hackett Publishing, 2001). Copyright © 1981, 1986, 1989 by A. C. Graham; preface to the 2001 edition copyright © 2001 by Hackett Publishing Company, Inc. Reprinted by permission of Hackett Publishing Company, Inc. All rights reserved.

Mencius, trans. with an introduction by D. C. Lau (Harmondsworth, Middlesex, Eng.: Penguin Books, 1970). Copyright © D. C. Lau, 1970. Reprinted by permission of Penguin Books, Ltd. All rights reserved.

♾ Columbia University Press books are printed on permanent and durable acid-free paper.

Printed in the United States of America

c 10 9 8 7 6 5 4 3 2 1

p 10 9 8 7 6 5 4 3 2

TO ROLF TRAUZETTEL

Teacher, mentor, friend

Contents

PREFACE
The *Philosophy* of the *Daodejing*   ix

CHAPTER ONE
How to Read the *Daodejing*

CHAPTER TWO
The Dao of Sex

CHAPTER THREE
Yin & Yang, Qi, Dao & De

CHAPTER FOUR
Paradox Politics

CHAPTER FIVE
On War

CHAPTER SIX
Masters of Satisfaction (Desires, Emotions, and Addictions)

CHAPTER SEVEN
Indifference and Negative Ethics   99

CHAPTER EIGHT
Permanence and Eternity   111

CHAPTER NINE
Death and the Death Penalty   121

CHAPTER TEN
"Without the Impulses of Man": A Daoist Critique of Humanism   133

APPENDIX 1
A Note on the Textual History of the *Daodejing*   147

APPENDIX 2
A Note on English Translations of the *Daodejing*   149

NOTES   153   INDEX   161

PREFACE

The *Philosophy* of the *Daodejing*

In a collection of essays on teaching the *Daodejing*[1] (or the *Laozi*, as I will call it here, if only for the sake of brevity), for which I was asked to write an introduction, several authors claim that this ancient Daoist "classic" is religious in nature and not, or at least not primarily, philosophical. I respectfully disagree with these opinions. I think that the text was initially (that is, in the fourth and third centuries B.C.E) a guide on what may be called "political philosophy" or, more specifically, a treatise on how to preserve or constitute order in society and, by extension, in the cosmos. Given today's historical evidence, it was not until the Han dynasty (206 B.C.E.–220 C.E.) that the *Laozi* became a cornerstone of religious activities and that religious Daoism "took off" as a social phenomenon.

Even if the *Laozi* is regarded as a philosophical text, readers sometimes complain that it is obscure and vague—and thus not very good philosophy. The text is often difficult to decipher and its terseness, as well as its "mystical" character, may make it seem impenetrable, particularly to those who expect clarity from a philosophical text. But that the *Laozi* is different in style and nature from contemporary philosophical writings should not prejudice readers. It stems from a time and culture that certainly did not produce any texts like "our" modern Western philosophical treatises. Still, in its own way and in the context of its culture, the *Laozi* contains a distinct and coherent philosophical "teaching." The present book is meant to expose this teaching, or at least some of its most important aspects.

Generally speaking, and quite different from the Greek philosophers, ancient Chinese philosophy was not so concerned about distinguishing what is true from what is merely apparent (or false) as it was with distinguishing order (*zhi*) from disorder (*luan*) and, particularly, how to bring about the former rather than the latter. Mencius (371–289 B.C.E. ?), a follower of Confucius, gives the following definition or "job description" of an ancient Chinese philosopher:

> There are those who use their minds and there are those who use their muscles. The former give order(s) [*zhi*], the latter are ordered. Those who give order(s) are supported by those who are ordered. This is a principle accepted by the whole empire.[2]

The Chinese word for "order" (*zhi*), when used as a verb, not unlike its use in English, also meant to give orders, and thus to rule. While rulers were actually in charge of bringing about order, it was, in the time of Mencius and the oldest extant traces of the *Laozi* (the Guodian manuscripts),[3] the philosophers' role to use their minds to assist the rulers in their efforts. The *Laozi* is no exception to this rule that, as it is evident from Mencius's statement, implied a rather unabashed "elitism." Like it or not, philosophy or intellectual activity in ancient China was distinguished from manual labor, and thus philosophical texts were not only political in nature (because they normally addressed the issue of good government and social order) but also "esoteric." They were not meant to contribute to general education, but to be studied only by a small fraction of the population, i.e., by those who had access to learning and power. If we want to understand the *Laozi* historically, we have to accept this context and thus also the fact that, as a philosophical treatise, it did not attempt to be generally accessible. It was originally a text for the few—and it clearly shows.

To approach the *Laozi* historically means that contemporary hermeneutical principles cannot readily be applied. As I attempt to show in the first chapter of this book, many of the assumptions with which we normally approach a philosophical text act as obstacles when reading the *Laozi*. It is not only "esoteric," it also has no identifiable author, no first-person voice, and it does not progress in a linear fashion. These characteristics require some degree of tolerance from the contemporary reader. The text is quite "outlandish" in its format, and if we only allow for "inlandish" styles of writing, the *Laozi* will always remain alien to us.

The *Laozi* is not only alien with respect to its form, its content is also rather "strange." Maybe even more unusual than its hermetic style are many of its doctrines. Most of the values and notions which we take for granted today cannot be detected in the *Laozi*. While it can certainly be read as a political text, we find nothing, for instance, about such concepts as "democracy," "liberty," "rights," or "justice." The political discourse of today bears little resemblance to that of China about 2,500 years ago. It is just as hermeneutically problematic to approach the text with a formal bias as it is to expect that it will fit seamlessly into today's semantics.

Does the fact that the *Laozi* was not written for "us" make it irrelevant? Does its study have only historical value? I don't think so. Just as it is important to study a foreign language to get a better understanding of one's own, it is important, in my view, to study a different way of philosophizing or thinking to better understand one's own reasoning. The *Laozi* is as truly challenging as a foreign language. It challenges one to think differently and to look from a different angle at what has become all too familiar. In some of the chapters of this book I have therefore included some contrastive analyses. The chapters on sex and time, for instance, try to explain how the philosophy of the *Laozi* differs significantly from dominating views about these issues in the Western tradition. Studying the *Laozi* "contrastively" may thus be an exercise in studying cultural contingencies.

Studying a text such as the *Laozi* does not only have the rather negative value of demonstrating that historically there were other ways of thinking. It can also have the value of introducing credible alternatives. The *Laozi*, for instance, provides views on such important issues as emotions, morality, death, and war—to name four topics addressed in this book—which may still offer something "positive" for contemporary readers. Perhaps the *Laozi*'s teaching of "indifference" can do something to alleviate the present-day tendency to "take sides."

The aspect of the *Laozi* that I find philosophically most interesting—and which is specifically addressed in the final chapter of this book—is its challenge of human agency. The modern Western philosophical tradition, which started off with the discovery of subjectivity, has been so focused on the ego and its powers that the position of the *Laozi* may be perceived as somewhat scandalous. Its maxim of "non-action" (*wu wei*) leads to a general view of the world—including human society—as a mechanism that is not so much based on individual activities as it is on a functioning which happens "self-so" (*ziran*) or spontaneously. It is this "autopoietic" alternative that I find exciting.[4]

I am indebted to Ryan O'Neill for proofreading the manuscript, suggesting many corrections, and mending my English.

The Philosophy of the *Daodejing*

CHAPTER I

How to Read the *Daodejing*

Darker even than darkness—
Gate of multiple subtleties
LAOZI I

The *Daodejing* or, as it was called earlier in history, the *Laozi*,[1] is a book that can both fascinate and trouble its readers. Many feel attracted and inspired by its "darkness." For some, this darkness appears as a depth that contains intellectual mysteries and wonders. To others, this same darkness appears as an obstacle to understanding. These readers find it difficult to make sense of the cryptic verses and vocabulary. They cannot detect anything truly enlightening in the text and find nothing of interest in the hidden and dark.

The "darkness" of the *Laozi* is partially due to the fact that long ago it changed from one type of text into another. Initially, the text was not written to be read, particularly not by readers of the twenty-first century. The *Laozi* is a collection of sayings that grew into its present shape over several centuries, and in its early stages it was transmitted orally rather than in writing. It seems that, originally, the text was neither intended to become a "book" nor to be read by those who studied it. It was to be recited, not perused.

The oldest manuscripts of the *Laozi*—written on bamboo or silk and unearthed only in the past few decades—have been found in tombs. They had been given to the dead not so much as reading materials but likely as signs of prestige and wisdom, as indicators of power and status for their passage into the world of the ancestors. Writing was done for ritual purposes, in these cases funerals, and funeral rites were the most elaborate and important type of rites in ancient Chinese society. In the *life* of Chinese antiquity, however, the *Laozi* was not present in the form of a book. Rather, it has to be assumed that it (or, more precisely, the sayings that later constituted it) was taught orally to those who had access to education, that is, the small privileged stratum of people who held social power and property. These people learned texts such as the *Laozi* by heart. Its poetic character, the political and philosophical content, and the historical background of the cryptic sayings suggest that they were transmitted from mouth to mouth within a cultural elite. In the time between the fourth and third centuries B.C.E., the *Laozi* was used by this group as a guideline for the exercise of social power, for the cultivation of one's body, and for attaining one's proper place within nature and the cosmos.

It is beyond doubt that the teachings of the *Laozi* belonged to the core patterns of orientations within which the ancient Chinese interpreted their position within the state and the cosmos. The teachings of the *Laozi* and other philosophical texts functioned as a general source of meaning. They provided a set of schemata with which the world could be understood, and, more importantly, that helped one to plan action in the world. Texts such as the *Laozi* are documents of the self-descriptions and self-prescriptions of Chinese antiquity. When we read such texts today, our reading differs considerably from how they were once studied. Our view of the world is not that of ancient China; consequently, the *Laozi*, printed as a paperback in English translation, is no longer the same as it was more than two thousand years ago. We perceive this text in an entirely different way than a member of the Chinese ruling class who tried to memorize it in a long gone age.

The *Laozi*, as we find it in a present-day bookstore, is no longer within its original cultural context. It is a kind of mummified transformation of a semantics—a network of meaning—that was once alive in a region which had practically no contact with the predecessors of what we call "Western civilization." Its semantic network of meaning that once was valid and revered (not only among the living but even, as it was assumed, among the dead) has now become obscure—and this is one of the reasons why the *Laozi* now seems dark and impenetrable to many of its readers.

Taking all this into account, it is clear that the *Laozi* cannot have many of the characteristics we have come to expect from a book:

First, the *Laozi* does not have an identifiable author. In this text there is no writer who expresses individual thoughts. We will be disappointed if we anticipate that the text will introduce us to an original "mindset." There is no specific person who addresses us. The "I" that we sometimes find in the text is not the ego of an individual who speaks to us and wants to convey some observations. It is rather a marker for the space that the potential reader—or better: listener—is supposed to occupy. The students of Daoist teaching can "insert" themselves and their ego into the text when the "I" is mentioned. In an anonymous way, the *Laozi* asks those who study it to identify with its teachings. These teachings are not brought forth as unique insights, they are rather introduced as the presentation of a general order.

Second, there is no topic that the *Laozi* systematically addresses. As a collection of sayings, it expresses its teachings in a fragmentary manner. Its "philosophical crumbs" are not arranged according to a specific pattern, there are no analytical steps taken to solve any explicit philosophical problem, there is no particular order of logical conclusions, no chain of arguments: There is no obvious point that the text aims at. Unlike the *Analects* of Confucius, there are no dialogues between a master and his students clarifying, in the question-and-answer format, philosophical terms or moral values. There is no discernable issue at stake, no obvious range of content; there is not even a general explanation of what the text is about. The reader certainly realizes that it is trying to convey something, but one is never quite sure what it is.

The *Laozi* is not a text written to be read in a specific sequence, it does not truly have a beginning and end, and it does not evolve along a certain pathway. The earliest manuscripts that have been excavated suggest that the materials contained in the *Laozi* were initially part of shorter collections (as in the Guodian texts) and arranged in different orders (as in both the Guodian and the Mawangdui manuscripts).² We are, nowadays, used to writing and books, and we have developed corresponding habits of reading. Such assumptions—for instance, that a text has a beginning and an end—were very uncommon in early Chinese antiquity. For the ancient Chinese, a text such as the *Laozi* "normally" existed not between the covers of a book but in oral recitation and in memory. The early manuscripts show us only how the text was buried and "mummified." They do not show us how the text was actually used in life—namely in the form of oral sayings of wisdom that had no strictly fixed order or sequential arrangement.

But how can the *Laozi* be read if it lacks an author, a clearly stated topic, and a beginning and end? How can it be read if it was not written to be read? Given its very peculiar form, the *Laozi* can hardly be compared with the traditional linear texts of our culture, such as books, essays, or speeches. In a certain sense it is, surprisingly, easier to compare it to nontraditional and nonlinear texts such as the so-called hypertext of the Internet. The hypertext of the Internet also lacks a specific author, it has no beginning or end, and it is not dedicated to the exclusive treatment of one specific issue.

As opposed to linear texts that unfold along a straight line of argument or plot, hypertext is of a complexity that cannot be disentangled—and it was never meant to be disentangled. The Web functions as a web, not as a thread. It has no true beginning (we can start "surfing" at any site) and no true end (because its content is continuously renewed and expanded).

The hypertext of the Internet functions like a bulletin board onto which new messages are constantly put while others are taken off. In the Net, the semantics of our society is caught. By communicating within the Net, just as outside of it, society builds its structures. Web sites, the little notices on the great board, are of a fragmentary nature. They contain dispersed and more often than not extremely condensed information that we, however, understand, because we are already familiar with their content. We are familiar with what we find on the Net because we know it from everyday life. Also, the Net is extremely repetitive. There is not one bank, one university, one newspaper, or one sports franchise on the Net—there are thousands and thousands of them. Each differs only in details. We are guided through the chaos of the Net by *links*, crossovers that lead us from page to page, from site to site. With their help we can find slight variations of the same information. The links lead us from one node in the Net to the next.

The brevity of many Web sites presupposes familiarity. Hypertext is a vast collection of more or less concise brochures that normally do not first explain what they are about. Hypertext is not a book and does not introduce the reader to its topic. Previous knowledge is assumed; the experienced "users" of hypertext are familiar with the terrain and surf from site to site without needing to be steered, guided, or instructed. They are already well acquainted with the topic and know what to expect.

Like many Web sites, the *Laozi* speaks anonymously. There is a lack of individual tone or a personal authorship in the multiple virtual postings. The messages are similar, but the messenger stays hidden or, rather, is insignificant. It does not really matter who exactly updated the text of this or that Web site. Similarly, for understanding a text like the *Laozi* it is often irrelevant to know who was responsible for a particular version of a particular chapter. This is demonstrated by the fact that in many cases, as on the Internet, "the "updaters" are not even known by name, and because no one is interested in keeping track of this kind of information, it soon becomes impossible to reconstruct a textual history.

As a text, the *Laozi* is so intricate that it can hardly be disentangled, and just like hypertext, any attempt to disentangle it would be out of place. The *Laozi* was never "completed." There is no authentic original version that can be discovered. It has no original order or sequence. The materials were put onto the "bulletin board" of the *Laozi* at different times in different forms and in different orders. They were rewritten, recomposed, extended, and abbreviated time and again over centuries until, at a certain point, they assumed a "standard" form that resembles our concept of a "book." However, this happened at a relatively late stage of its textual history and does not represent the nature of the text in its formative period. In the earlier stages of its history, particularly in the four or five centuries preceding the common era, the *Laozi* functioned less as a book and more as a kind of ancient hypertext, as a textual *gestalt* that was in a continuous process of construction and deconstruction, of growth and reduction.

Like many of the concise texts on the Internet, the chapters of the *Laozi* tend to repeat slight variations of a theme without giving an explicit explanation of what this theme means. The experienced "user" of the *Laozi* already knew what the issue was so there was no need for a prior initiation. The repetition of catchwords, of *termini technici*, and the establishment of a jargon is typical for a discourse of the already initiated. Those who "surfed" the *Laozi* in ancient China were familiar with its semantics. This semantics did not have to be elucidated in detail, it was simply used and reused.

The links that enable one to move, not from site to site, but from chapter to chapter, and from verse to verse, within the *Laozi* are, of course, not electronic signals but, rather, rhetorical ones. The bridges that connect the chapters and verses of this "chaotic," disorderly text, the hinges that keep the text together and constitute its unity, are the expressions and phrases, the images and symbols, and the strategies and maxims that repeatedly occur in close succession. The "networking" in the *Laozi* is done linguistically. Every chapter refers to others by the use of the same or similar metaphors, by repeating, in slight variation, similar mottos, and by applying the same set of vocabulary.

When one takes a closer look at the *Laozi*, it turns out to be an endless chain of rhetorical connections, a network of related sayings, a collection of associated images and instructions. The obscurity of the text vanishes when one follows these links and traces the repetitions and variations. If the chapters are read on their own, or the book is read linearly, the text remains hermetically closed. But if one adopts a different reading strategy and treats the *Laozi* as a kind of hypertext, as a collection of nonlinear but still tightly connected materials, then the "darkness" lightens and the *Laozi* indeed becomes a "gate of multiple subtleties."

One can begin to explore the *Laozi* by starting at any chapter or verse. In the following I hope to show how a randomly chosen starting point can lead to references and connections to practically all other chapters and sections—and thus the "networklike" structure of the text should become obvious. It is quite impossible, however, to follow *all* the "links" of a given verse or line. This is a task that can hardly be completed because of the more or less endless possibilities for detecting interrelations between passages. Moreover, trying to do so would soon become extremely repetitive since the *Laozi*'s stock of images, symbols, strategies, and instructions is rather limited. The links of the *Laozi*, the motifs and mottos that guide the reader through the text, are, more often than not, variations of the same.

My starting point for the following journey through the *Laozi* is chapter 6:

> *The spirit of the valley does not die—*
> *This is called: dark femininity.*
> *The gate of dark femininity—*
> *This is called: root of heaven and earth.*
>
> *How ongoing!*
> *As if it were existent.*
> *In its use inexhaustible.*

These are certainly some of the "darker" verses of the "dark" *Laozi*. This is due to the fact that we find here, packed together within a few characters and words, a number of core images that lack further clarification or explanation. Still, sentence for sentence and word for word these images can be taken as "links" that lead one into the metaphorics and rhetorics of the whole *Laozi*, and it is only within this larger context that they become meaningful.

The first verse of the sixth chapter has, in my translation, seven words. In the Chinese original, however, there are only four characters: "valley spirit not die" would be a literal translation. This extremely concise saying begins with an image—the "valley spirit"—and this image is then associated with a specific quality, namely immortality. Obviously, the core image in this line is the valley, and the valley is said to have some sort of "spirit" that seems to be integral to it as a kind of virtue, strength, or power, like, let's say, the "American spirit." I will argue that the "spirit" of the valley is due to the structure of this image. This is to say that the valley shares a certain structure with other images in the *Laozi* that have a similar "spirit" and similar characteristics. It will be seen that the valley is one of several images that share a similar nature.

The valley is referred to as possessing a specific quality. This quality expresses a certain effect that is attributed to it and goes along with its structure: imperishability. This connection will prove to be typical for the rhetorics of the *Laozi*: Certain images share similar structures, and because of these structural similarities, they also share similar characteristics and a certain efficacy. These two elements together, structure *and* efficacy, can be understood as an implicit or explicit instruction or as a strategic guideline: If one acts in accordance with the structure of these images, certain characteristics or qualities will necessarily go along with it, and therefore one will be able to produce specific effects and evoke a specific efficacy. The image is thus a visualization of a strategy for action and behavior, it shows how certain results can be achieved. In this way, the first line of the sixth chapter already contains the three basic elements that constitute the rhetorics of the *Laozi*: *images*—and their inherent structures—are combined with certain qualities or an *efficacy*, and the image and its efficacy together teach a *strategy*.

What kind of image is the "valley," what is its structure? If one conceives of it as a "link" that connects to other images in the *Laozi*, one can soon discover its makeup and its meaning. The valley is also mentioned in chapter 15. There it is said:

> *How raw!*
> *Like uncarved wood.*
> *How impenetrable!*
> *Like muddy water.*
> *How vast!*
> *Like the valley.*

In this passage the valley is paralleled with two other images: uncarved wood and muddy water. (The words for these images rhyme in Chinese—this phonetically highlights their parallelism.) As Wang Bi (226–249 C.E.), the famous editor and commentator of the *Laozi*, remarks, these three images share one trait: they are all void of a particular, positive form or shape. They are all, so to speak, "negative" shapes. The uncarved wood is not yet shaped—it is still raw and without a discernable form. A similar negativity can be ascribed to the muddy water. While water in general lacks a specific shape—and therefore can take on any shape—muddy water is a "chaotic" mass of particles that have not yet settled. This water will clear up and then take on a specific color and quality, but as of yet it is still in a primordial "non-form" that precedes its actual form. The valley, in the context of these images, seems to be an image of emptiness, of space that is not yet filled. It is "vast," a vast and empty space. It is a negative form, as opposed to the "full" mountains that surround it. It is without content or positive features. It is mere potential, a potential that has not yet materialized.

The valley is, in the context of chapter 15, obviously one image of "featurelessness" among others, and one could now further trace these images through the *Laozi*. Instead of turning to the uncarved wood and the muddy water, however, I will follow the valley and, as a first result, conclude that it is an image of negativity, emptiness, and the unformed. The valley thus seems to represent the *void* that precedes actualization.

In chapter 28 the valley is mentioned again, and it is again spoken of in connection with the "uncarved wood:"

> *Be the world's valley,*
> *and constant efficacy will suffice.*
> *When constant efficacy suffices,*
> *you will return again to the state of uncarved wood.*

The valley is here said to be of "constant efficacy." This "efficacy" or "power" (*de*) seems to be its fertility. The valley is a place of fertility, and this fertility is constant. Every year the valley lets things grow. The valley is also, naturally, a river valley. Therefore chapter 41 says:

> *Higher efficacy resembles the river valley.*

Chapter 39 refers the reader back to that quality of the fertile river valley which was the starting point for our present excursion—emptiness:

> *The river valleys are not to be already full,*
> *lest they may be exhausted.*

The negative qualities of the valley, its emptiness and featurelessness, let it possess the positive quality of fertility. This nurturing "power" ascribed to it by the *Laozi* is immediately related to its being without form, to its being mere potential. That which itself is without shape allows that which has shape to take on shape. And, as chapter 39 says, the emptiness of the valley guarantees its inexhaustibility. That which is empty cannot be emptied. The valley is an inexhaustible spring of fertility precisely because it has no positive features. Emptiness, durability, and fertility are interconnected. This interconnection leads us directly back to our starting point in chapter 6: "The spirit of the valley does not die."

The *gestalt* of the valley—a negative, merely potential, and imperishable void—can lead the reader to a couple of other similar images that share the same characteristics. The image of the valley in chapter 6 serves not only as a link to other mentionings of the valley or the river valley in other chapters, it also serves as a link to other images of the same structure. Such a similarly structured image is the bellows in chapter 5:

> *The space between heaven and earth—*
> *Does it not resemble a bellows?*
> *Empty, but not consumed,*
> *The more it is moved, the more comes out.*

Just like the valley, the bellows is also "empty, but not consumed." For both, their emptiness is the condition for their being inexhaustible. The empty cannot be used up. At the same time, this emptiness represents continuous fertility: something always comes out of it. In perfect analogy to the productive emptiness of the valley and the bellows, chapter 11 introduces a number of other images:

> *Thirty spokes are united in one hub.*
> *It is in its [space of] emptiness,*
> *where the usefulness of the cart is.*

> Clay is heated and a pot is made.
> It is in its [space of] emptiness,
> where the usefulness of the pot is.
> Doors and windows are chiseled out.
> It is in its [space of] emptiness,
> where the usefulness of a room is.

Here, the images of the wheel, the pot, and the room are associated with the same qualities as the valley and the bellows. The wheel's hub is a hollow space that cannot be worn down and still continuously enables the wheel and the cart to run smoothly. The pot too functions like a valley: its empty middle makes it a vessel. The empty middle can hold anything and can never be used up. It is continuously "refreshed" when we change the contents of the pot. Doors and windows allow us to use our houses and rooms, but they, being mere holes, will never be "exhausted," no matter how often we use them. All these images embody the "spirit of the valley" that does not die. The valley is an untiring source of life, the bellows and the hub are untiring centers of continuous movement; the emptiness within the pot, the window, and the door cannot be diminished or exhausted by any amount of use.

The image of the valley in chapter 6 is thus first a link to other chapters and verses in which it literally reappears, but it is also a link to images that function analogously. Because these images share a common structure, all these can in turn be understood as links leading the reader to more abstract illustrations of the same structure. At the end of chapter 11, the structure of the preceding three images (and, implicitly, also that of the valley and the bellows) is summarized in these words:

> Thus,
> there is presence [you] for the benefit,
> there is non-presence [wu] for the use.

All these images are images of efficacy, they show how something works. In every case the efficacy is based on the combination of emptiness and fullness, of "having" and "not-having," of "presence" and "non-presence."

The valley consists of empty space surrounded by the "full" mountains, the door consists of empty space surrounded by wood, and so on. Also, these images highlight the inexhaustible usability of the emptiness that is the condition for the permanent "benefit" of the different things or "scenarios." In order to bring about permanent functionality, these images say, there has to be a structure that effectually integrates emptiness and fullness, or presence and non-presence.

In this way, there is now, proceeding from the image of the valley, a third level of potential "linkage" that leads us through the *Laozi*. In addition to the repeated use of analogously structured images, what can also count as a link is the mere mention of the basic structure itself. The image of the valley in chapter 6 refers, first, to other valley images in the *Laozi*, it next refers to similar images, and third, it refers to the mentioning of the common structure of all these images. In this structural perspective, the image of the valley refers, for instance, to chapter 40. Here, instead of using images, the *Laozi* speaks on an abstract level of presence and non-presence as such.[3]

It is possible to follow this path of abstraction even one step further and discover a fourth level of "linkage." Presence and non-presence, or emptiness and fullness, are obviously the two structural components that constitute a number of concrete images in the *Laozi*. Sometimes these structural components are not illustrated in the form of images, but reappear in the form of *abstract symbols*. Such "dry" symbols, void of any concrete imagery are, in the *Laozi*, numbers. This becomes clear in chapter 42[4] when the "ten thousand things" are portrayed as resulting from "one," "two," and "three." In this way, even such an abstract chapter as chapter 42 is just another possibility for expressing "the spirit of the valley."

Our look at the variations and abstractions of the image of the valley shows clearly, as stated above, that they are normally related to certain *effects*. The efficacy of the valley is its ability to continuously produce life. This very effect, the effect of inexhaustible usefulness, was attributed to a variety of images and structures—and this proves that these do not merely represent but rather *demonstrate* something. They are repetitions of the same *instruction*. They all say: If you are able to establish a scenario or a behavioral pattern in accordance with this structure of efficacy, if you are able to act in accordance with these structural components, then you will be able to bring about the corresponding results and "benefits." All the images are illustrations of productivity, productivity in life (valley), movement (wheel, bellows), or function (windows, doors). Therefore they are not merely meant for contemplation, but for practice. They are lessons for acting and behaving, they are learning materials for strategic training.

The first line of chapter 6 has thus revealed itself as a strategic maxim that is reflected again and again throughout the *Laozi* in various sayings and mottos. The phrase "the spirit of the valley does not die" does not particularly belong to this chapter alone. It resonates with many other verses and lines and can be associated and evoked when reading any chapter. The text is constructed in such a way that what one finds in one chapter connects with what one reads in others. The textual elements are constantly varied and echo each other. On principle, one could fit them in anywhere in the book.

So far we have identified a number of images and structures that directly parallel the verse on the valley in chapter 6. This verse can, however, not only be understood as a link to analogously constructed sayings and phrases, it can also serve as a link to more indirectly related passages. The image of the valley evokes, for instance, the image of a river; the fertility of the valley is due to the water that runs through it. The relation between the valley and the river leads to a wider array of images of a larger topical group. The image of the valley is part of the "image family" of water that figures so prominently in the *Laozi*.

We only have to return to chapter 28, which the image of the valley has already led us to, to see that the valley and water are not only in nature but also in the *Laozi*, immediately connected. This chapter not only says "Be the world's valley, and constant efficacy will suffice"; it also says, in perfect parallelism:

> *Be the world's river*
> *and constant efficacy won't leave.*

The "constant efficacy" of the valley that lends it its fertility is that of the river—the valley and the river are inseparable. If one is supposed to be a "valley" to the world (i.e., the source of its flourishing), then one is likewise supposed to be a "river" to the world. The images of the valley and the river (or other bodies of water) are obviously connected and are used in conjunction. Chapter 66 begins:

> *Rivers and oceans*
> > *are able to be king of hundreds of valleys*
> > *because they have the goodness to lie lower than those.*
> *Exactly therefore*
> > *they are able to be king of hundreds of valleys.*

The dales are once more "topped off" by the rivers and oceans because their waters are even lower. The fertility of water functions upward, from bottom to top. It originates from below. Thus the ocean is privileged over the valley; it is, in comparison to the valley, the "king." One could now start a journey through the *Laozi* and, beginning with the valley, pass through all the rivers, the oceans, and various other bodies and qualities of water. One would find, next to the "nourishing goodness" of water (ch. 8), all kinds of useful effects. For instance, its softness is of such endurance that it conquers the hard (ch. 78).

One might object that water imagery would ultimately lead us astray from our starting point in chapter 6 since there is no literal mention of it in these lines. But this is not really true. Even though water is not literally addressed in chapter 6, it is implicitly present. This is how the chapter continues after "The spirit of the valley does not die:"

> *This is called: dark femininity.*

The connection between the "spirit of the valley" and "dark femininity" is elucidated in chapter 61:

> *A large state is*
> > *low lying waters*

> *the female of the world*
> *the connection of the world.*

The identification of water and the feminine is based on their common quality of being fertile and their association with "conception." Water "chooses" the lower position, and the more powerful a body of water is, the lower it lies. The lowest lying body of water "conceives" from everything above its level. By being able to conceive from everything else, the lowest lying body of water is, naturally, the most fertile. It is the ultimate pivot within the cycle of reproduction. All life-giving energy flows down to the lowest body of water. But this body does not keep this energy for itself, it transforms it into the nourishing power for the "ten thousand things" to grow. The same pivotal position within the cycle of life is obviously ascribed to the "feminine." In the reproductive process of nature, water and the feminine take on the central position that combines conception and nourishment.

The function that water and the feminine are ascribed in the biological realm is supposed to be taken on—in the words of chapter 61—by the "large state" in the political world. This state is supposed to bring together the resources of the world, as the chapter continues to explain, to "nourish the people." The natural circle of reproduction is an immediate model for social order. In nature, water and the feminine provide "the connection of the world," in society it is provided by the "large state" or the sage-ruler. This connection is the point of "reversal" within the productive cycle—and this is, as chapter 40 says, the very "movement of the Dao."

The structural characteristic of femininity is, in perfect analogy to water, its pivotal position in the course of life as a connection and a point of reversal between conception and birth. (This structural characteristic is, as another link, naturally connected to the image of the mother, particularly in chapter 52.) The structure and position of the feminine corresponds to the quality of lying low as well as to the "spirit of the valley." Therefore, the permanence and continuity ascribed to the valley are likewise ascribed to the feminine. Just as the structure of emptiness and fullness constitutes the ongoing functioning of the valley, so the structure of the low and the high associated with the feminine and water constitutes an enduring pattern of production. Once more, the imagery establishes a *structure* that is associated with certain *characteristics* and serves as a *strategic* model.

In chapter 6, the structure of the feminine has another quality: it is "dark" or "hidden" (*xuan*). This darkness or concealment—this invisibility—serves as a link to chapter 51:

> *Generating without possessing,*
> *Acting without depending,*
> *Rearing without ordaining:*
> *This is "dark efficacy."*

Darkness or "hiddenness" is a female quality—and thus a quality of the power to generate. Generation, the turn between conception and birth, happens in "darkness," it is hidden from sight. Since it cannot be observed it is without a specific form. The very center and turning point of generation does not take on shape. It is "hidden," "obscure," or "dark"—as the term *xuan* can be translated. The feminine stands for this turning point where there is no longer and not yet form. The dark and hidden center of generation allows for things and beings to grow, but it does not show itself in that which grows. Water nourishes the plant, but it does not become visible in the plant. The place of "reversal" is without contours; while it brings forth shapes and forms it does not possess any itself. It also does not impose any specific appearance on that which it produces—everything that is born looks different. The "dark efficacy" produces a multitude of shapes and forms. This is so, once again, both in nature and in society. A truly productive ruler will also be "dark," "hidden," or "obscure."

Chapter 6 then continues by introducing another image:

> *The gate of dark femininity—*

The image of the gate obviously relates to the image of the valley. It shares the structure of an emptiness surrounded by a fullness that establishes a pattern of efficacy. The image of the valley has already led us to the image of "doors and windows" in chapter 11. Obviously, the door and the gate are parallel images. In connection with the imagery of water and femininity, however, the gate not only associates utility but also fertility and biological generation. The feminine embodies the process of conception and birth that passes through a "gate." The images of the valley, the female, and the gate in chapter 6 are mutually explanatory, they belong together. The image of the gate combines the two structures of emptiness/fullness and low/high: it is emptiness in the midst of fullness and the passage between high and low. As the "gate of dark femininity," it is here the gate of conception and birth. This very same imagery appears in chapter 10:

> *When heaven's gate opens and closes,*
> *can you be the female?*

"Heaven's gate" in the *Laozi* is certainly not the Christian door to an eternal paradise but rather the gate of nature in a much more literal sense. It is the gate of conception and birth in the midst of nature's process. The Chinese term for heaven (*tian*) is therefore also often translated as "nature." "Heaven" is not something *trans*cendent, not something *beyond* or *after* this world, but the center of the world's functioning. Heaven is the course of the celestial bodies and thus the course of the seasons and the course of time itself. It is the cycle of life that life passes through. Within the natural process of growth and withering, the most crucial position is the position of the "gate," this empty and invisible space of femininity. The opening and closing of the gate of generation constitutes the cycle of conception and birth, giving and taking, the coming in and going out of life.

Chapter 6 adds another image to the "gate of dark femininity." It continues:

> *This is called: root of heaven and earth.*

The image of the root connects with the image of the gate—and the two words (*gen* and *men*) rhyme. Understood as a link, the image of the root leads to chapter 16:

> *The things in the world are manifold,*
> *they all return again to their root:*
> *"stillness."*

The root is the hidden part of the plant that remains in darkness. It is unseen because it is covered by the earth. Plants grow from their root. In fall and winter, when the plants wither, they return to their root, and in spring a new plant emerges and takes on a new shape and form. It is clear that the image of the root repeats all the imagery that precedes it in chapter 6. The root lies low, and thus it both receives and generates life, it is the "dark efficacy" in the midst of the life cycle of the plant. It guarantees the constancy of the plant, even though the parts that are seen are not themselves constant. The root is the turning point, the point of reversal in the life of the plant which is invisible and not manifold, as opposed to the manifold "things" that it generates time and again. The root itself is still and unmoved, it does not change, it is the constant center of a process of change.

The root is called the "root of heaven and earth" in chapter 6. This connects it to "heaven's gate" in chapter 10. The root and the gate represent the natural "opening and closing" of life. They are also related to the bellows in chapter 5. The bellows was an illustration of "the space between heaven and earth," empty and continuously pulsating and generating. The root, the gate, and the bellows all depict the structure of natural or "cosmic" fertility.

The remaining verses in chapter 6 further comment on the preceding images and, moreover, provide further linkages to other chapters in the *Laozi*:

> *How on-going!*
> *As if it were existent.*
> *In its use inexhaustible.*

The natural processes of the valley, the gate, and the root are "ongoing." The Chinese word for "ongoing" alludes to a thread, and this "ongoing" also has the connotation of "going through." The valley, the gate, and the root are not "fully" there. They are, so to speak, "empty there" or, as the text puts it, "as if it were existent." The center of the proceeding is empty—a passageway that is non-present, but by no means absent. This "in-between" type of existence of the non-present is also alluded to in an exclamation in chapter 4:

> How deep!
> And seemingly there.

The root is deep and seemingly there. We cannot see it, but it seems to be there. That which is hidden from sight or empty or without form still somehow exists. It is a "deep" or "obscure" way of existing, a non-presence in the midst of presence. In addition, as chapter 4 also states, and in the case of so many natural settings and human artifacts, the non-present is the inexhaustible source of utility:

> The Dao is empty,
> and when it is made use of, it still does not become full.

At this stage it should be sufficiently clear how the *Laozi* can be read: Chapter 6 is an assembly of images. It starts with one image, and then adds others that connect to it. But one does not have to read the chapter in a linear way: Each line and image connects to a number of similar lines and images throughout the entire book. The whole text is a sequence of images presented in no particular order but with nearly inexhaustible possibilities for intertextual linkages. When reading the text, one cannot expect the next line or chapter to say something entirely *new*. One should rather expect a further variation of what is already supposed to be known, another depiction of what has been depicted before. None of the images in the *Laozi* can claim an absolute priority over the others. There is no one image that introduces the rest. One can practically start anywhere in the book. It is, however, important to realize how the images mutually explain and relate to each other. While the order of the text is arbitrary, the images themselves are not. Reading the text can thus be an experience of transforming that which seems to be "darker than darkness" into a "gate of multiple subtleties."

In summary, the images that one encounters in the *Laozi* often turn out to be illustrations of *structures* (such as emptiness/fullness, low/high) that have certain *qualities* (permanent, productive). In this way, they serve as illustrations of *strategies*. They are instruction models for achieving efficacy.

By tracing the literary links provided in chapter 6, I hoped to show a way of reading the "obscure" *Laozi*. This hermeneutic exercise is, of course, not only a methodological game—it also implies an interpretation of the text and, particularly, of its core notion, the *Dao*. If the *Laozi* introduces one illustration of a structure of efficacy after the other, then the Dao "itself" may be exactly this: a structure or order of efficacy. The Dao of the *Laozi* seems to be the "way" (this is the literal meaning of the word) that processes (or mechanisms or organisms or things) function when they function well. The images show that this model of efficacy is not limited to a particular realm. It is applicable to nature or the cosmos as well as to social or political issues. It applies to agriculture, government, and also artisanship. It may be taken into account when growing and nourishing plants and animals, when ordering a community, producing things, or, in general, when living "between heaven and earth."

I believe that the images of the *Laozi* strongly suggest that the Dao, as a structure of efficacy, was believed to consist in the interplay between two aspects: emptiness and fullness, or non-presence and presence, or, likewise, constancy and change. Within this structure, emptiness was to hold the central position—but only to allow for the fullness of change to take place around it in an orderly, rhythmic, and ongoing fashion.

CHAPTER 2

The Dao of Sex

The *Laozi* talks about sex, and it does so frequently. It talks about sexuality because the Dao, as a "way," is a way of living and dying. It is also a way of fertility. As such, there is a sexual dimension to it and, accordingly, a number of poetic images in the *Laozi* are directly or indirectly sexual. Images of motherhood and femininity—for instance in chapter 6: "The spirit of the valley does not die / This is called hidden femininity"—are immediately related to sexuality and reproduction. Chapter 28 connects the image of the fertile and "female" valley by speaking of the river that runs through it:

> *Know the masculine and maintain the feminine—*
> *be the world's river.*

The "river" of the world is the source of its fertility—all life emerges from water. The river, as the spring of life, is here paralleled with the twoness of the sexes. It encompasses the masculine and the feminine. Obviously, the structure of fertility requires a united duality. If one wants to understand how a continuous process of production and reproduction is possible, one has to know about sexual duality. The unity of becoming and passing away also has a dual structure, and this is what the above quoted lines allude to.

Reproduction is the result of the conjunction of the sexes, and to be able to come together they have to be different. The sexual distinction between masculinity and femininity is manifested by different but complementary characteristics. Chapter 61 says:

> *The female overcomes the male*
> *by constant stillness.*
> *Because she is still*
> *she is therefore fittingly underneath.*

Obviously, these lines are about sexuality. In sexual intercourse—at least from a Daoist perspective—stillness and movement come together. Male sexuality goes along with movement, and female sexuality with stillness. This distinction is accompanied by a second one, a distinction of positions. The female is suited for the lower position while the male is suited for the higher one. But in the Daoist context, this distinction by no means indicates a subjection of femininity. The opposite is the case. In Daoist imagery—and especially in the *Daodejing*—the lower position is both more prestigious and mightier than the higher. That which lies low holds power. This is why the female overcomes the male in the performance of sexual intercourse. The male exhausts himself and loses his life energy, which is in turn absorbed by the female. In stillness, the female "acts without acting"—just as prescribed by the famous Daoist maxim "*wei wu wei*." By not acting she takes the male's energy and becomes the place of fertility that produces life.

In this way, chapter 61 of the *Laozi* provides a background for the later male Daoist practice of holding back semen in sexual intercourse. By preventing an ejaculation, the man learned not to squander his energies but rather to concentrate them within his own body. The retention of semen was supposed to increase male power and potency. Sexual intercourse was perceived as a kind of sexual struggle lost by the male partner, and accordingly—from a male perspective—a strategy had to be to adopted that had female qualities. This included the reduction of movement and averting of ejaculation. In the sexual struggle, the winner was not the one who fecundates, but rather the one who managed to be fecundated and thus to give birth.

The imagery of chapter 78 in the *Laozi* also seems to indicate a "struggle of the sexes." The first two stanzas are:

> Nothing in the world
> >   is smoother and softer than water;
> > but nothing surpasses it in
> >   tackling the stiff and the hard,
> > because it is not to be changed.
>
> That water defeats the solid,
> That the soft defeats the hard:
> >   Nobody in the world who does not know this,
> >   but still nobody is able to practice it.

I do not think that one has to be a Freudian to detect a sexual meaning in these verses. In the *Laozi*, and in Daoism in general (as well as in many other traditions around the world), images of femininity and water are immediately connected with each other. Their connection is due to their common characteristic of being fertile, which is *the* sexual characteristic *per se*. Chapter 61 already alluded to their common qualities when it spoke of that which lies low. When chapter 78 describes water as the smooth and soft element that attacks the stiff and the hard and thus "defeats the solid," it also suggests a sexual interpretation of the same imagery. In the sexual act, the female triumphs not only because she lies low and still but also because she is soft and remains unchanged. This is opposed to the higher and moving male who lets himself be changed into stiffness. Everybody in the world, as the text reminds us, knows about this; however, there is hardly anyone, or more precisely, any *man*, who consequently practices the different "female" sexuality of stillness and retention. This line resonates with the line in chapter 28 that asked the reader to know the male but maintain the female.

In the *Laozi*, sexual intercourse is a competition of the sexes won by the female. This is described as an obvious fact; however, it is not well understood. In real life, men usually do not alter their behavior and continue their sexual strategies of activity, rigidity, and "lying on top." Daoist sages, on the contrary, will be aware of the struggle of the sexes and the resulting structure of sexual intercourse. They will "know" the male but "maintain" the female. Therefore, the ideal Daoist man is neither a sexual athlete nor a womanizing macho man; he rather resembles a human figure that precedes virile masculinity—he resembles an infant. The Daoist superman is a baby:

> *One who holds the fullness of efficacy*
> *is like an infant.*

Chapter 55 begins with these lines and continues to describe the sagelike Daoist child:

> *Bones and muscles are soft and weak—*
> *but the grip is firm.*
> *He does not know about the union of the male and the female—*
> *but the penis is erected.*
> *This is the maximum of Qi.*[1]

The Daoist infant "does not know about the union of the male and the female." He is presexual or not yet sexually active. This sexual non-activity of the male infant proves that it "knows the masculine" but "maintains the feminine." The infant maintains the female traits of softness and weakness in his muscles and bones—simultaneously, he has a permanent erection. But since he does not "know about the union of the male and the female," he does not lose his potency. The infant never ejaculates. Therefore, as the text says, "it holds the fullness of efficacy" and maintains "the maximum of Qi." The Daoist boy applies the "female" strategy of non-action, stillness, and of "lying low." Chapter 28 says:

> *If the continuing power does not leave you,*
> *you return to the state of infancy.*

The Daoist infant serves as an illustrative image to the reader (or listener) of the *Laozi*. By following its example, one will retain and thus increase one's energies, powers, and efficacy. By following this *Dao* of sex, one will maximize one's *De*.

One could object that if everyone followed this example there would be an end to all fertility, to all reproduction. Fecundation would never take place, and the cycle of reproduction would come to an end. Such an objection, however, overlooks a crucial aspect of the *Laozi*. It was not meant to be studied by everyone. It was composed, in the strict sense, for only one type of person: the Daoist sage-ruler. Daoist sage-rulers act without acting. While they remain totally passive, all activities in society go on without disturbance or interference. Their non-action is paralleled by the perfect action of all others—*wu wei er wu bu wei* ("non-action, / but nothing is undone"), as chapters 37 and 48 say. The non-active Daoist ruler is at the center of the perfect Daoist society. Similarly, the non-sexual Daoist sage is at the heart of Daoist sexuality. The sexuality of the Daoist sage is represented by the maximum of potency of the male infant whose penis is erected but who does not ejaculate, and who—as an infant—precedes the distinction of the sexes as it is manifested in the sexual act. This sagelike infant affirms and enables all sexual activity even though (or just because) he himself is sexually inactive. He thus resembles the Daoist ruler who, by being inactive and indistinct, affirms and even enables all the distinct social activities.

The sexual abstinence of the Daoist sage is therefore essentially different from, for instance, Christian chastity. The sexual abstinence of the Daoist sage is utmost sexual latency and potency. It is the "root" (to use another important Daoist image) of Daoist fertility and reproduction. This sexual abstinence is not against sexuality, but rather the paradoxical anchoring of the sexual in the non-sexual.

The Dao is the continuous process of growth and withering, of becoming and passing away, and thus it is also a sexual process, a process that entails the division of the sexes and their "struggle" for fertility. This struggle is depicted as a natural contest that leads to procreation by the triumphant female. With female fecundation the contest ends—and begins anew, because fecundation is the turning point at which new life and new sexuality arise. The cycle of sexuality is based on duality and on change, but it is also dependent on something unchanging for its permanence— just as the turning spokes of a wheel are dependent on the hub and the bellows is dependent on its empty center (to use two other images from the *Laozi*). The Daoist sage, as depicted by the presexual infant, embodies the empty center of the sexual cycle, the non-sexual potency in between sexual activity, a never-exhausted spring or root of fertility.

The Dao of sex in the *Laozi* is not predominantly a Dao of human sexuality. Since this is the case, it is not concerned with *gender* issues. The sexes are, from its perspective, not *socially* but *cosmically* defined. It is not the distinction between men and women that serves as the guideline. When the *Laozi* speaks of the masculine and the feminine, such as in chapters 61 and 28, it does not mean *men and women* in particular but the masculine and feminine in general. The Chinese words *pin* and *mu* (in chapter 61) and *xiong* and *ci* (in chapter 28) were normally used in the realm of fauna. Daoism does not look at the world from an anthropocentric perspective, and this is also true for its view on sexuality. Human beings are sexual beings, but their sexuality is only part of a larger sexuality that encompasses all of nature. The best-known Chinese metaphor for human sexuality expresses this non-anthropomorphic way of thinking: it is called "the game of clouds and rain" (*yunyu*). Sexuality takes place within a cosmos of sexuality. Sexuality is not only not confined to human beings, it is not even confined to the realm of the biological in a modern scientific sense. Everything between heaven and earth takes part in processes of growth and withering. This applies not only to humans, animals, and plants but also to "non-organic" things such as the four seasons, the weather, and stones. From this perspective, in other words, everything that "is," "becomes," or is "produced." The term *sheng*, which is often translated as "life" or as "to be born," is not limited to the biological world. The cycle of the "five phases of change" (*wu xing*) is a cosmic cycle of fertility that describes the general order of fertility or "birth." The whole cosmos is a continuous process of fecundation and birth, and within this process

THE DAO OF SEX   27

the art of "wind and water"—or *Fengshui*—illustrates at which times and locations things will best "grow."

Since human sexuality is not essentially different from "natural" sexuality, it is neither good nor bad. It is in no way better than the copulation of animals, it simply produces new life. There is nothing sinful or "dirty" in human sexuality either. There is also nothing particularly "satisfactory" about it, and so there is a lack of a semantics of "sexual fulfillment" in the *Laozi*. Human sex is not so much human as it is simply natural. That the Daoist sage is depicted as a presexual or sexually inactive infant does not imply that sex would morally spoil him. The infant's sexual inactivity is only an aspect of its general inactivity, of its *wu wei*. The sexual inactivity of the Daoist sage is not an evasion of a presumably "brutish" sexuality. It is rather, as stated above, a paradoxical affirmation of a thoroughly sexual cosmos.

The *Laozi*'s non-anthropomorphic concept of sexuality allows for "sexual" interpretations of passages that, at first sight, do not seem to have sexual content. Chapter 23, for instance, talks about a "thunderstorm" and a "whirlwind." These events are portrayed as untimely and unproductive natural "outpours." They seem to be, so to speak, the premature ejaculation of the weather. Early emissions of energies lead to disaster and catastrophe. Even in regard to the intercourse between heaven and earth there has to be caution. If everything between heaven and earth holds on to its position and goes along with the rhythm of natural change, then the cosmic begetting and conception will be in tune. Chapter 23 of the *Laozi* describes how the intercourse between heaven and earth may result in a "harmonious giving and taking" that in turn produces fertility and procreation. This cosmic giving and taking encompasses not only mankind but everything under heaven.

Sexuality and procreation emerge when there is a duality of giving and taking. The male and the female are the two elements that constitute this continuous *way* (or Dao), and they rest on or circle around a central unity—which is a dual unity. This unity is represented by the image of the Daoist sage—the presexual infant that contains, without waste, all potency in itself.

This image of the infant corresponds to other images in chapter 28 that can also be read sexually. The second part of this chapter says:

> *Be the world's valley*
> *and constant efficacy will suffice.*
> *When the constant efficacy suffices,*
> *you will return again to the state of uncarved wood.*

The image of the valley represents fertility and emptiness. The valley manifests the unity of the two fertile slopes that surround it. Like the image of the jug, or the image of the wheel, the image of the valley represents the Daoist structure of productive order: an empty center surrounded by a full and useful periphery. The valley, like the infant, precedes sexual duality. It is the asexual unity that is at the heart of sexual duality. The river that runs through the valley nourishes the procreation of everything that grows on the two slopes. The image of the Daoist infant thus corresponds to the valley and to the river. One should here remember that chapter 28 begins with the phrase: "Be the world's river." The images of the valley and of the river are supplemented by the image of the uncarved wood. This image can also be understood in a sexual dimension. The same "constant efficacy" and unsquandered potency that characterizes the infant, the valley, and the river is also ascribed to the "state of uncarved wood." The uncarved wood is also, in a way, presexual. It has not yet taken on a specific form and so precedes duality. *Laozi* 28 ends with the words:

> *When the uncarved wood is parted,*
> *then tools come into being.*
> *When the sage makes use of them,*
> *he becomes the leader of all officials.*
> *Well, great woodcarving does not carve anything off.*

The uncarved wood represents the state before sexual separation, the state of unity. Once the wood is parted, "tools" come into being, and these tools are used in the house and in agriculture. They are the tools that are used by men and women in their work. Thus, these tools are also images of femininity and masculinity. The male and the female, in turn, are the two most general "tools" of both society and procreation. Daoist sages precede duality and make use of tools without squandering anything, without carving anything off. They constitute the unity of the duality. They themselves are asexual but affirm and constitute sexuality.

The Dao is the unity that simultaneously precedes and latently contains sexual duality. It is therefore not only portrayed as the "mother" (see chs. 20, 52, 59) but also, as in chapter 21, as the "father." Being presexual, the Dao can be both father or mother. Chapter 25 begins:

> There is a thing—
> it came to be in the undifferentiated
> it came alive before heaven and earth.
> What stillness! What emptiness!
> Alone it stands fast and does not change.
> It can be mother to heaven and earth.

Chapter 25 speaks about the presexual, preseparated Dao that "came to be in the undifferentiated" (*hundun*). It precedes the duality of heaven and earth which are the masculine and the feminine partners of the cosmos. Heaven and earth are the man and woman of the cosmos, and the Dao is still and empty. It precedes their separation. It is the not-yet-sexual mother of all mothers, the not-yet-sexual father of all fathers. The image of the male infant with an erected penis and the image of the cosmic mother both illustrate this sexual dimension of the Dao.

That the variety of images in the *Laozi* are either directly or indirectly related to fertility and procreation sufficiently proves that sexuality was an important topic in early Daoism. At the same time, it is also quite remarkable that this theme is more or less void of erotic connotations. This is primarily demonstrated by the fact that the *Laozi* is much less about human sexuality than it is about natural or cosmic sexuality. Contemporary semantics usually associates the notion of "erotic" with humans and not with animals or clouds and rain. "Eros" has to do with human values such as pleasure, aesthetics, or lust and thus connects sexuality, culture, and morality. Such an erotic dimension of sexuality is hardly found in the *Laozi*.

The non-erotic representation of sexuality in the *Laozi* becomes quite obvious when it is compared with the representation of sexuality in ancient Greek philosophy, particularly in the works of Plato. One of Plato's most important dialogues, the *Symposium*, is more or less exclusively about *Eros*. The varieties of ancient Greek positions on eroticism that are displayed in the *Symposium* are, however, so complex that I cannot discuss them here in detail. I will concentrate only on a few aspects that I find particularly relevant in comparison with the *Laozi*. These aspects are the views that the *Symposium* ascribes to Eryximachos and Socrates.

Eryximachos is a medical doctor and thus a man of science. To him, erotics is effective everywhere in the world. He conceives of it as a kind of principle of conjunction. Love is the art of conjoining and incorporating in both nature and culture. For instance, in the composition of music sounds are conjoined into a harmonious whole. To Eryximachos, there is a good and a bad Eros. Accordingly, all things can be conjoined either in a bad or a good way. In the case of a good conjunction, there is productivity and fertility, and in the case of a bad conjunction there is disharmony. When a good Eros prevails in nature, the weather and the climate will be good and favorable. Consequently, the seasons will harmoniously follow each other. But when a bad Eros prevails, the stars will be in disarray and so will the seasons. This will lead to disorder, to catastrophes and, in a certain sense, to sexual diseases in nature. Eros and love are for Eryximachos general forms of ordered or disordered constellations, and these may be constellations in the cosmos, in nature, or in human society.

Socrates has a very different understanding of Eros. To him, human love and human erotics are, in their pure forms, the striving toward a union with the good: "Thus, all in all, love aims at the good that one always wants to have" (206a). Love is a particular desire for the good. It aims at the *production* of the good through the union with the good. Love is fertility, conception, and creation, and all this "within the beautiful." Human beings strive for a union with the beautiful, to make themselves immortal through this union and thus acquire godliness. In bodily, loving union with the beautiful (the beautiful women), new life is created and the immortality of the human race is realized. In this way, humans partake in divine eternity. For Socrates, the striving for physical procreation and immortality is surpassed by the striving for spiritual procreation and immortality. The "Platonic" love between men makes use of the soul's fertility. This mental capacity of procreation is of a higher value than mere physiological procreation. True philosophers will direct their capacities for procreation beyond the bodily realm toward the transmission of wisdom, virtue, and justice. For Socrates, erotics leads beyond the physical into the realm of the good, the true, and the beautiful. It leads toward spiritual immortality. Thus Socrates concludes that "it will not be easy to find better support for the human nature than Eros" (212b).

It is easy to see how Daoist sexuality, as it is presented in the *Laozi*, is at odds with the Platonic conception of erotics. While common Western notions of erotics are more in line with the "humanist" and "cultural" position of Socrates, the Daoist "cosmic" concept of sexuality bears more affinity to the pre-Socratic "cosmic" erotics of Eryximachos. There are many similarities between Daoism and the Greek pre-Socratics, and this again seems to be the case with respect to concepts of sexuality.

In line with Eryximachos, sexuality in the *Laozi* is not particularly human. It is, on the contrary, a certain "drive" that functions throughout the entire cosmos. For both Eryximachos and the *Laozi*, sexuality is a nonpersonal process that can either go on orderly or not. A disorderly cosmic "sexuality" has nothing to do with moral shortcomings but with breaches of the natural order. Just as the *Laozi* describes thunderstorms and whirlwinds (ch. 23) as kinds of sexual malfunctions in nature, so Eryximachos names weather or natural phenomena such as hailstorms and mildew as indicators of a disorderly cosmic Eros. For both of them the order of the heavenly bodies and the seasons is immediately related to fertility and procreation.

As opposed to Eryximachos, as well as to the *Laozi*, the Socrates of the *Symposium* no longer conceives of erotics as a nonpersonal cosmic sexuality in the sense of an ongoing mating of complementary aspects for the sake of fertility and procreation. For Socrates, Eros and sexuality are set apart. Nonhuman sexuality is no longer part of the Eros that is discussed by Socrates. Here, even the physical aspects of human erotics play only a minor and less valuable role. For him, true love and a true Eros transcend bodily concerns. In its highest form, the Socratic Eros has nothing to do with the conjunction of the male and the female. It becomes a "trans-sexual" and "trans-bodily" love for the sake of divine beauty, virtue, and truth. Such an intellectualization and humanization of sexuality—the concept of a "Platonic love"—is completely alien to the *Laozi*.

The *Laozi* does not share the Socratic Eros's overcoming of the physical—that, in some of its later Christian adaptations, could turn into a total devaluation and denial of the body, a sexual "ethics" that damns human "flesh" and its activities. In the *Laozi* there is no special emphasis on human sexuality, and thus no particular concern for such all-too-human (and thus all-too-narrow-minded) categories as sexual "sin"—or, conversely, "gratification." Also, the sexuality that appears in the *Laozi* is free from aspirations toward the divine. Sexuality in the *Laozi* is not transcendent: it leads neither beyond the body nor beyond the mundane. With Socrates and Plato, Western philosophy established a distinction between sexuality and the Eros. Such a distinction, as far as I can tell, was not made in the *Laozi*. Here, the Daoist sage attempts to reach a presexual state of highest sexual latency that precedes the division of sexuality into the sexes. The Socratic-Platonic philosopher, on the other hand, aspires to transcend sexuality and enter into a realm of a "spiritual" and "divine" Eros.

CHAPTER 3

Yin & Yang, Qi, Dao & De

The preceding discussion of sexuality has, hopefully, shown that the early Daoists conceived of the world as a permanent process of production, as a cycle of fertility. To keep this process going, it is essential to follow the course or order of "nature." If this order is violated or if one acts contrary to it, disasters and catastrophes may follow. Such a conception of a natural world-order or course of (re)production is not something unique to the *Laozi*. One may well find comparable views, for instance, in ancient Greece, and particularly in pre-Socratic thought. Still, the *Laozi* expresses its conceptions of a natural order in the language and context of ancient Chinese philosophy. The *Laozi* shares its vocabulary with other schools of thought such as the Confucians, the Legalists, and the Mohists. The concepts discussed in this chapter—such as Yin and Yang, Qi, Dao and De—were generally used by all these schools. They were not unique to the *Laozi*, but common to the philosophical discourse of ancient China.

The world of sex in the *Laozi* is a world based on distinctions (male/female) that, nevertheless, constitute a unity, an integrated process. In the ancient Chinese terminology the two basic elements of (sexual) twoness are Yin (the female aspect) and Yang (the male aspect). The unity of these two aspects is the Dao. This basic structure appears in many ancient Chinese philosophical texts, though most notably in the *Book of Changes*; it serves as a kind of fundamental pattern for various cosmological and other speculations. It is an elementary part, so to speak, of the grammar of ancient Chinese philosophical semantics.

One of the best-known chapters in the *Laozi* is the forty-second. It is the only chapter in this text where the terms *Yin* and *Yang* are used. It says, somewhat cryptically:

> *The ten thousand things;*
> *carrying Yin, embracing Yang—*
> *blending Qi to create harmony.*

The "ten thousand things" are simply the different kinds of things and beings, they are all the things that are present (*you*) between heaven and earth (*tian di*). The constellation of the ten thousand things and the way they "interact" seems to be ordered or organized by a very basic distinction, which is designated by the terms *Yin* and *Yang*. In chapter 42, Yin is depicted as "carrying," and that which carries is below that which is carried. Lying low, it corresponds, as far as the imagery is concerned, to the female. It is complemented by that which it is embracing. This, in turn, may be regarded as that which contains latency or potency and thus is connected to the imagery of the masculine. The Yin/Yang distinction, however, is not to be reduced to or simply identified with the femininity/masculinity distinction, and much less with the distinction woman/man. It is a much more *general* distinction than these, and the two sexes are only one of its (most important) manifestations. The Yin/Yang distinction is, in the terminology of the sinologist Marcel Granet, a distinction of the "rubrics" by which everything that is or happens can be classified. It provides the most basic structure into which the world can be divided and, consequently, by which what goes on can be explained.

According to Marcel Granet, the terms *Yin* and *Yang* can be traced back to, among other things, the distinction between the shadowy (Yin) and the sunny (Yang) sides of a hill.[1] In addition to femininity/masculinity, the Yin/Yang distinction thus also corresponds to the distinction darkness/brightness and, more specifically, to the moon and the sun. Many very common words in the contemporary modern Chinese language still reflect this wide pattern. The sun is called *tai-yang*, which literally means "highest Yang"; and if the weather is overcast, the Chinese speak of *yin-tian*, which literally means a "Yin-sky." The sexual dimension of these words is reflected in many biological and medical expressions such as *yin-dao* (literally, "the path/way of Yin") for vagina, and *yang-wei* (literally, "Yang-weakness") for impotence. Yin and Yang are thus very concretely the two rubrics for "interaction" in the realm of the "ten thousand things." A hill on which things grow is divided into a sunny and a shadowy side. These sides correspond to the division between light and darkness, sun and moon, and again correspond to the division between male and female that characterizes biological life. The division of the biological sexes is one dimension of the rubrics of reproduction, and the division of time is another. In this sense, not only do biological "beings" have two sexes, but also the course of time and the celestial "bodies" as well. The course of time, the sun and the moon, are, in fact, from this perspective as "biological" and as "bodily" as plants, animals, and humans. Time and "body" are two inseparable aspects of *the same* basic distinction that allows a process of fertility and life to go on. The Yin/Yang distinction structures human life as well as agriculture and the course of time. It is the distinction at the heart of cosmic life or, in the poetic language of *Laozi* 42, at the heart of "creative harmony."

In his discussion of the rubrics Yin and Yang, Marcel Granet points to a very important line that appears in the later parts of the *Book of Changes* (*Yijing*).[2] This line simply says: "One Yin, one Yang: this is called Dao."[3] Yin and Yang are not forces or substances, but rather complementary aspects or *moments* that constitute any orderly, efficient, and "creative" process. As Granet explains, they are "elements of a set of conceptions which is dominated by the idea of rhythm."[4] Granet—whose work directly influenced the "founder" of structuralism, Claude Lévi-Strauss—describes in great detail how, in ancient Chinese thought, the two components of Yin and Yang constitute the rhythmic structure of the cosmos. The sun and the moon, the male and the female, are merely examples among the ten thousand things that rhythmically interact in accordance with this structure. This rhythm is one of change and exchange, a rhythm of harmonious mutual complementation. Yin and Yang constitute the rhythm of the *Dao*. They are the two most basic segments of time, but not of time as a "transcendental" cognitive or "subjective" pattern in our mind or as an "objective" category in physics. They are, rather, like day and night, male and female, that which literally *comes and goes (together)* when the way of time, and thus life, proceeds.

In chapter 42 of the *Laozi*, the harmonious and creative rhythm of Yin and Yang goes along with "blending Qi." The term *Qi* (or, in other transcriptions, *Ch'i* or *Chi*) designates something like the universal or cosmic "medium" in ancient Chinese thought. Everything that is present somehow consists of Qi. This Qi, however, is, unlike some pre-Socratic models, neither conceived of as atomistic—it is not constituted by small particles—nor as elementary—it is not constituted by one or more basic "stuff(s)." Qi is neither material nor ideal in nature. This distinction, which was quite important in ancient Greece (and most notably in Plato), is not made in the *Laozi*. It may rather be understood as some sort of medium or energy. In this way, it faintly resembles science's conception of light, which also cannot be sufficiently explained as "matter."

The word *Qi* is, similar to the terms *Yin* and *Yang*, not a highly "scientific" term. It was, and still is in contemporary Chinese, a rather common expression. In this respect it is comparable to the English word *matter*, which is also used in a number of colloquial ways (such as, for instance, in the expression "What's the matter?"). This exemplifies how in Western languages some philosophical and scientific terms have made their way into common language and thus shape linguistic habits and a commonsense understanding of the world. Through its usage in colloquial language we are so used to the notion of "matter" that we normally do not question it. Similarly, the notion of Qi has been used in a large number of ways throughout history and represents a very general and common understanding of the world or cosmos which is, maybe somewhat surprisingly from a Western perspective, nevertheless nonmaterial. Qi is, for instance, used in words for "air" (*kong qi*; literally, "Qi of the empty space") or "gas" (*qi-ti*; literally, "Qi-body") as well as "smell" (*qi-wei*; literally, "Qi-smell," or "Qi-taste"). In this way, the weather is *tian-qi* ("the Qi of the sky"), *Qi-fen* ("Qi-atmosphere") is the word for "mood," and a bad odor is called *chou-qi* ("stinking Qi"). To be able to deal with Qi properly and, more important, effectively is the art of *Qi Gong*. This is literally the "exercise of Qi," which is now becoming increasingly popular in Western countries. Qi is not only in "nature," it is also in works of art such as paintings and poems, it is in houses and gardens, in interpersonal relations and emotions like love and hate, and it is also important in warfare. Because of this, I call it a sort of general or universal "medium."

Yin and Yang, the two basic moments of the cosmic rhythm, are also the two basic aspects with respect to Qi. Ancient Chinese philosophy also spoke of them as the "two Qi" (*er qi*). When the Yin-Qi and the Yang-Qi blend nicely, as described in chapter 42 in the *Laozi*, then there will be harmony. If there is order in the basic "medium," then good results are to be expected. Thus, one always has to ensure that the Qi "energies" are interacting in a positive way and in correspondence with the rhythm of Yin and Yang. This is, for instance, a main principle in traditional Chinese medicine. Qi is also the medium of the body, and bodily cultivation is consequently the cultivation of Qi in harmony with the order of Yin and Yang. Daoist bodily practice therefore stresses the importance of breathing exercises in which Qi, as "air" and "energy," is rhythmically inhaled and exhaled. Thereby, the flow of Qi can be brought in harmony, and the body—as a process—can be stabilized. Many techniques of *Qi Gong* are related to breathing and aim at optimizing the circulation of Qi in and around the body. Such exercises were obviously already practiced at the time the *Laozi* was composed. Some passages, like the following in chapter 10, allude to them:

> *When you concentrate the Qi and attain softness,*
> *can you be like an infant?*

Here, we find once more the image of the infant (which, being soft, also connects to the images of water and the female) as an illustration of an organism that truly embodies an ideal state of "concentration." Nothing in this tenth chapter suggests that this concentration is to be understood mentally or spiritually (as the word *concentration* is often metaphorically used in English). In the context of known Daoist practices, it is rather to be assumed that the "concentrating" of the Qi is a bodily exercise that may include some form of (rhythmic) breathing. In this way the Qi may literally circulate around a center such as the heart (which, as the term *xin*—meaning both "heart" and "mind"—suggests, had also been taken to be the location of consciousness).[5]

The concentration of the Qi that leads to a harmonious flow around the heart and within the body should not be forced. In ancient Daoism, Qi exercise seems to follow the maxim of acting through non-action (*wei wu wei*). It is not an exercise, like gymnastics, where one forces the body to assume all sorts of "unnatural" positions which require a great deal of "strength." Daoist (breathing) exercises rather attempt to let the Qi "naturally" take on a rhythmic pattern or flow. Chapter 55 in the *Laozi* says:

If the heart directs the Qi, this is called: forcing.

Daoist Qi exercise does not use coercion. Cultivation, be it bodily or political, is never forced. Instead, order is attained by not meddling with things. The infant symbolizes this attitude. It is a human being that, presumably, does not willfully or with "subjective" intentions direct its body or mind. It certainly moves and has consciousness activity—but it does not yet try to actively control its body and mind. It allows the Qi to unfold unimpeded. The Daoist Qi exercises and breathing practices attempt to reestablish the state of the infant.

Qi is the energy or the general medium with and in which the ten thousand things move and change. It characterizes and "defines" the realm of things and events. Everything that has a form or a shape, all that happens or behaves, takes on its *gestalt* through Qi. As the universal medium of all things, forms, and events, Qi is therefore necessarily also within the realm of the distinct and within the rhythmic rubrics of Yin and Yang. The cosmic course consists of darkness and brightness, male and female, growing and withering. The Yin-Qi and the Yang-Qi are the two moments of this course. The world of Qi is also the world of the Yin/Yang distinction. As such, it is the world of all that is present (*you*). All the ten thousand things, in their presence, are present within the rhythm of Yin and Yang in and as Qi. Accordingly, they have specific Yin/Yang and Qi characteristics and can thus be qualified and classified. They are not empty or void.

The distinction between empty and full is also the distinction between non-presence (*wu*) and presence (*you*). One may think once more of the images of the valley and the bellows. The fullness of things moves or grows around a central element of emptiness. The bellows can "breathe" rhythmically because it is hollow, and the rhythmic growth and life processes in the valley depend on the empty space in its midst. The realm of distinction, and thus the realm of Yin/Yang and of the corresponding Qi, is dependent on a central unity—which is in itself indistinct. It is only through the indistinct non-presence in its midst that the presence of the distinct can exist. The world of fullness, the rhythmic, productive, and fertile flow of Qi—or, life (and death)—is in turn based on the "nothingness" of that which has no qualities and no characteristics. The ten thousand things, the Yin/Yang distinction, and Qi constitute the realm of presence (*you*), but this is not all there is. Within presence there is also non-presence, as chapter 40 of the *Laozi* famously declares:

> The things of the world are generated from presence [*you*].
> Presence is generated from non-presence [*wu*].

In addition to the distinct realm of presence, the "things of the world," there is also non-presence. With the help of the Daoist image of the infant, we may say that non-presence precedes the dual and distinct world of presence just as the presexual being precedes sexual division. The pure potency of distinction is itself not yet distinct. Non-presence is the unity that precedes and "generates" the present things in their distinctness. This relation between presence and non-presence leads us back to the first few lines of chapter 42. It is, in numerical terms, a variation of the lines of chapter 40 quoted above, a variation that has "oneness" for non-presence, and "twoness" for presence:

> *The Dao generates Oneness.*
> *Oneness generates Twoness.*
> *Twoness generates Threeness.*
> *Threeness generates the ten thousand things.*

Oneness is the immediate "product" of the Dao—it is thus, as unity, at the "beginning" of the cosmic process. It is the foundation of twoness, the basic duality (Yin/Yang) that constitutes the rhythm of the cosmic course. In the body, the (empty) heart constitutes physical oneness while the life of the body consists in a process of twoness as manifested, for instance, in breathing-in and breathing-out. The twoness and "fullness" of the flow of Qi has the oneness and emptiness of the heart at its center. The same structure applies to the cosmos in general. Oneness is empty and non-present, but it is that which allows twoness to proceed. Oneness (indistinct non-presence) and twoness (presence, Yin/Yang distinction) add up to threeness. The threeness is thus "generated" by the integration of oneness and twoness. It is this threeness that opens up the world of multiplicity, the world of the ten thousand things. This "integral" mathematics shows that what is envisioned here is not really a "historical" process of linear causation or generation, not a diachronic development, but rather a process in which all elements combine into a synchronic order. Oneness, twoness, threeness, and multiplicity do not follow each other in a sequence, they rather go along with each other. In English we can paraphrase the chapter in this way: "With the Dao, there is oneness; with oneness, there is twoness," and so on. These moments coexist and are codependent, they do not represent an evolutionary history.

The oneness of the Dao has two aspects to it. It is both an internal and an external unity. On the one hand, oneness is at the center of that which functions well. For example, the body has only one heart, a wheel has only one hub, and a state has only one ruler. This aloneness of the center is the first and internal aspect of cosmic unity. The "solitude" of the center provides for the completion of a process or function—the single heart or hub unites the multiplicity of the bodily organs or the spokes into one mechanism or organism. The elements combine into one "scenario," one

Dao. The inner unity of the scenario is at the same time also that which makes the functioning a unit. The Dao is based on unity, and this unity is both the internal unity of the empty center and the external unity of the whole function. As a number, "one" symbolizes both the empty center and the full whole. It stands for both *singleness* and *totality*. This twofold symbolical meaning of the number one is important for reading and understanding chapter 39 in the *Laozi*:

> *Of those who once received oneness:*
> *heaven received oneness—to be clear;*
> *earth received oneness—to be at rest;*
> *spirits received oneness—to be animated;*
> *valleys received oneness—to be full;*
> *lords and kings received oneness—to set the world straight.*

Heaven and earth, the world of men, (ancestor) spirits, and nature all function well because they have attained oneness—in the double meaning explained above. The inner oneness—the empty space in the valley, the single ruler, and so on—constitutes the outer oneness of the "full" valley or the political community. The ruler, for instance, needs those to his "left and right," his ministers and subjects, to be a ruler. The inner unity provides a point of balance for the twofold moments that constitute the whole scenario. The outer unity is the unity of the harmonious combination of the twofold. The unity is always a unity of the twofold and the multiple. Chapter 34 says:

> *The Dao—*
> *How it flows!*
> *Left and right it can be.*

Here the Dao is once more depicted by the image of flow which, of course, is associated with the image of water. The Dao is the unified flow that extends to the left and to the right of a center which combines this "dual" flow into one.

Once an effective proceeding or scenario, be it social or natural, is established with inner and outer "oneness," it functions as a Dao. It is a

Dao that has its particular efficacy. This efficacy is named in the title that the *Laozi* was later given: "The Classical Scripture of Dao and De" (*Daodejing*). It can also be translated as "The Classical Scripture of the Way and Its Efficacy." *De* is the efficacy or "power" (as it can be translated as well) of *a* or *the* Dao. Many chapters in the *Laozi* speak about this efficacy of the way. Among them is chapter 54, which connects to the lines from chapter 39 quoted above. This connection is, first of all, topical. Chapter 39 spoke about the oneness in a number of different realms, such as the natural, social, and "spiritual." In chapter 54 the reader learns that once a perfect scenario is established in these realms, it will not fail to function with efficacy (*de*). The connection between the two chapters is, as we will soon see, also linguistic. Chapter 54 says:

> *When cultivation reaches the body,*
> *efficacy will be genuine.*
> *When cultivation reaches the family,*
> *efficacy will be abundant.*
> *When cultivation reaches the village,*
> *efficacy will be lasting.*
> *When cultivation reaches the state,*
> *efficacy will be rich.*
> *When cultivation reaches the world,*
> *efficacy will be broad.*

Efficacy or De will spread wherever things are arranged according to the ideal structure of the Dao. This begins with the body, and it extends to the family and the whole community until it reaches the whole cosmos. (The same concept of an ever-extending cultivation is also very important in Confucianism.) In the state, for instance, the good ruler will be able to rule and create order by means of his De, which we could here translate as "charisma" or, perhaps better, "prestige" (or "virtue," as it is also sometimes translated in association with the premoralist understanding of the Latin word *virtus*, which meant [male] power). In this way, De is the aura of a perfect functioning. In this sense, De is also some sort of "gift" (in the double meaning of this word, as a present and a talent) that comes along with the Dao. It is that which is *received* by the scenario that follows the Dao. The *Laozi* sometimes plays with the words for "to receive" and "efficacy" because they are both pronounced *de* (but are written with different characters). This word provides the linguistic link between chapters 39 and 54. Chapter 39 spoke about natural and social complexes that had "received" oneness and thus the structure of the Dao to function well. That which "receives" (*de*) the Dao and its inner and outer unity will at the same time have the gift of efficacy (*De*). Chapter 23 in the *Laozi* plays with the same two words. (I have, however, here chosen to translate *de* in the sense of "to receive" with "taking" to highlight its relation to the word "giving," which is used in connection with it in this passage):

> *What takes its way accords with the way,*
> *what takes accords with taking,*
> *what gives accords with giving.*

These lines (which have also been discussed in my chapter 2, on sexuality, in this volume) describe the Dao in terms of a rhythm of giving and *taking* (*de*). An efficacious (De) way (Dao) or proceeding consists in the harmonious play of these two moments. They are the aspects of production and reproduction. Chapter 60 has the following to say about the sage-ruler who, in accordance with the Dao, watches over the world:

> *Well,*
> *two do not harm each other.*
> *Thus efficacy is exchanged and returns to him.*[6]

By following the Dao, the sage-ruler is able to order the world of twoness. Thus the distinct aspects and moments do not strive to harm each other, but instead cooperate as a mutual giving and taking. This leads to a fruitful (and rhythmic) exchange of efficacy. This efficacy (De) was initiated by the ruler, and because it unfolds in society and brings the community to fruition, it will "return to him" in the form of increased "prestige" (De). Even he receives what he gave.

In their broadest dimension the Dao and its efficacy De are "at work" in the whole world. The ancient Chinese usually spoke of the "universe" as *tian*, which is often translated into English as "heaven." Used in this way the term *tian* does not only denote the actual sky above our heads (which is the concrete meaning of *tian*) but, as a *pars pro toto* expression, the cosmos. Still, the ancient Chinese concept of "heaven" is quite different from its "capital H" Christian counterpart. It does not indicate a transcendent realm where God dwells. It is not some paradise "beyond" from which the world "below" is somehow cut off. As *tian*, the Chinese concept of heaven designates the world in its entirety, including the "secular," or, rather, without any distinction between the secular and the sacred.[7]

In their concise—and highly recommended—"glossary" on important philosophical terms in the *Laozi*, Roger T. Ames and David Hall give the following explanation of the meaning of *tian*:

> The God of the Bible, sometimes referred to metonymically as "Heaven," *created* the world, but *tian* in classical Chinese *is* the world. That is, *tian* is both *what* our world is and *how* it is. *Tian* is *natura naturans*: "nature naturing." The "ten thousand processes and events (*wan wu*)," an expression for "all things that are happening," are not the creatures of a *tian* that stands independent of what is ordered; rather, they are constitutive of it. On this basis, *tian* can be described as the emergent orders negotiated out of the dispositions of the many particulars that are constitutive of it, human beings being no exception.[8]

Accordingly, in ancient Chinese philosophy "heaven" often designates how the "ten thousand things" (as the term *wan wu* is mostly translated) interrelate and, particularly, how they function and go on. Heaven is thus the pattern that is inherent in the cosmos. In Daoism, the term is closely related to "Dao." It is, for example, what can be seen when we look up: the movements of the heavenly bodies, the course of the moon and stars. But "heaven" is likewise present in the sequence of the seasons, in the weather, and in all kinds of natural phenomena, be they productive or disastrous. Heaven is thus not merely a spatial concept, it is not space in the sense of "outer space." It is rather, like the Dao, understood in terms of a process. It is the universe not in the sense of extended matter, but in the sense of a mechanics. As we will see, when heaven, as a process, follows the Dao, there will be order. But when it does not, there will be natural catastrophes.

To heaven belongs all that is "under heaven" or *tian-xia*. *Tian-xia* is therefore often translated as "world." The "world" is the concrete realm of the ten thousand things which function "under heaven," i.e., literally all that which, along with the course of the sun and the moon, is dark at night and bright at day. Heaven and that which is "under" it are inseparable. Human society is, of course, an important part of that which is "under heaven." Before electricity, we (unavoidably) slept at night and worked during the day. Being under heaven, people had to act in accordance with it.

In line with most other ancient Chinese philosophical texts, the *Laozi* generally recommends, when under heaven, to do as heaven does. It particularly discourages any actions that would try to go against the heavenly mechanics. Such actions are doomed to fail, or at least to be strenuous and exhausting—ultimately they cannot be effective. The most efficient way to act is to act in line with heaven. Chapter 68 says (in Mawangdui version B):

> *This is called: matching heaven.*
> *It is the ultimate of antiquity.*

To "match heaven" is depicted as a most ancient time-honored ideal. It is implicitly suggested that one return to this simple but valuable strategy. The order of heaven is simply there—and has always been. All that humans have to do is to act "sparingly," as chapter 59 points out:

> *For ruling men,*
> *for serving heaven,*
>   *nothing compares to being sparing.*

To bring about order among humans it is best to follow the Dao of heaven. Heaven itself acts "sparingly," so to "serve" heaven is to not take any action against it. Heaven has no specific aim and no specific intentions of "where to go," and the same should apply to the ruler. Heaven is not selfish. When selfishness is eliminated, things will go on smoothly. Chapter 9 says:

> To withdraw oneself when the work proceeds—
> this is the Dao of heaven.

The Dao of heaven is the largest dimension in which the maxim of "doing the non-doing" (*wei wu wei*) applies. Personal, selfless withdrawal is at the heart of a frictionless performance, the only performance that works out well. Chapter 73 provides some examples of this "Dao of heaven":

> The Dao of heaven—
> Without battling, it is good at winning.
> Without speaking, it is well responded to.
> Without calling, it is approached spontaneously [*ziran*].
> Being at ease, it is good at planning ahead.

The Dao of heaven "takes it easy," as easy as it gets. It does not develop an urge to impose itself on anything—because it has no self. Neither does it compete nor command. Since this is the case, every response to it is completely unforced, it is a natural, "self-so" (*ziran*) resonance. Since nature itself does not call upon anything or anybody, the things in nature follow nature naturally. When the night comes, the flowers close themselves "spontaneously"—the night does not have to tell them to do so. This most effective way of governing is the way heaven governs all that is "under" it.

While the Dao of heaven happens unintentionally and selflessly, it still acts rhythmically. The "aimless" course of the days and seasons is harmonious. This is described in chapter 77:

> The Dao of heaven is like flexing a bow:
> what is high is lowered,
> what is below is lifted,
> where there is abundance, there is taken away,
> where there is a lack, there is added to.

The flexing of a bow was a movement of reversal, just like the movement of the Dao. After the shot, the bow again takes on its initial shape. One may think back to the image of the wheel. It also functions through such a movement of reversal. There is a continuous exchange of high and low as the spokes rhythmically change their respective positions. This change is to the benefit of all that participate in it. Chapter 81 says:

> *The Dao of heaven*
> *benefits without doing harm.*

The Dao of heaven comprises both heaven in the sense of the "sky" and the earth. The expression "heaven and earth" (*tian di*) is often used synonymously with "heaven" (*tian*). To speak of "heaven and earth" in conjunction makes it even more obvious that the cosmic or natural process is one of "response," that it is a dynamical process that involves the "matching" of elements, the harmonious blend of aspects or moments. The efficacy of this process is measured according to its ability to continue itself. A well-established rhythmical process is able to go on (possibly) without end. Chapter 7 in the *Laozi* states:

> *Heaven is enduring;*
> *the earth is long-lasting.*
> *The reason why heaven and earth*
>   *can be enduring and long-lasting*
>   *is that that they do not live for themselves.*
> *Therefore they can live enduringly.*

The selflessness of heaven and earth allows them to carry on their mutual giving and taking without harming each other. Because they have no specific "agenda" they do not conflict with each other. They treat each other sparingly, and thus their interchange produces no friction. Since there is no friction, the process does not lose any energy and does not cease. Cosmic "interaction" is action without action and therefore it can be permanent. The same rules of frictionless action can apply to all dimensions, macrocosmic and microcosmic, within nature or "under heaven." Chapter 25 in the *Laozi* shows how these dimensions are intertwined as elements of one continuous "machinery":

> The Dao is great.
> Heaven is great.
> The earth is great.
> The king is also great.
> In the land there are four greats—
> and the king positions himself where they are one.
> Man follows the earth as a rule.
> The earth follows heaven as a rule.
> Heaven follows the Dao as a rule.
> The Dao follows its "own course" [ziran] as a rule.

The Dao is the general cosmic course. Next there is heaven and what is "under" it, namely, earth and men. All these dimensions are integrated into one another, they are different levels of an "organic" or "mechanic" process. The process is also "centralized" and revolves around the center that provides its unity. The ruler of men has to manifest this center in society. His central position within the state reflects the cosmic balance that is dependent on such a centric arrangement or constellation. The Dao is the most general term for the integrated order of cosmic and social processes—it is itself neither beyond these process nor actively initiates them. It just follows its "own course" (ziran) or, literally, it is "self-so." It does not have an external cause and does not impose itself on the "lower" dimensions. The only "rule" of the Dao is to let things happen as they happen by themselves. It is not a "cosmic" law or principle that precedes the world like a plan precedes an action or a blueprint precedes a building. It is the immanent order in the course of things.

Ideal rulers will act in accordance with this "non-rule" of the Dao. They will just allow the "own course" or "self-so" of events to unfold. Chapter 64 says about the Daoist sage-ruler:

> He is able to support the own course [ziran] of the ten thousand things,
> and does not dare to act on them.

To rule is also to restrain oneself. One first has to master oneself in the sense of diminishing one's personal intentions in order to allow everything to function on its own. The effects of such a mastery are described in chapter 17 of the *Laozi* when it describes the rule of the best of all rulers:

> *The work is completed,*
> *the tasks are followed,*
> *and all the common people say:*
> *"It happens to us 'self-so' [ziran]."*

Under the perfect rule of the sage, people will do their respective duties without coercion. They will do "naturally" what has to be done. Thus they will feel some sort of "lightness of being." They will perform their tasks just as the heavenly bodies move along their courses or the grass grows and withers. They just do what is theirs without any conspicuous effort. This is the effect of *ziran*, of things happening "self-so" and taking their "own course."

Nature and "civilization," the universe and society, function best if they function like a perpetual motion machine, a machine that follows its own course without the input of any external energy or the loss of energy due to internal friction. Any mechanism that is dependent on an external source of energy, on a cosmic battery, so to speak, will expire along with its battery. Only the self-sustained mechanism that is totally immanent can be absolutely free of exhaustion. If an organism is totally closed and "self-so" it cannot "leak." Its power or efficacy is unobstructed. This is, from the perspective of the *Laozi*, the ideal scenario for both the cosmos and the state. Chapter 51 says:

> *Therefore*
>   *the ten thousand things honor the Dao*
>   *and cherish the De (efficacy).*
> *Honoring the Dao,*
>   *cherishing the De:*
>   *none is rewarded for this,*
>   *so it happens constantly "self-so."*

There is no "reverence" paid to the Dao or the ruler in the Daoist cosmos or state. This would disturb the absolute immanence of the scenario. There is no external origin or source, no active power that "guides" the process. The elements within the perfect mechanism certainly "cherish" their unobstructed "lightness of being"—but there is nothing and nobody discernible whom they have to thank. The people in the perfect state will cherish and honor their ruler just as all things in nature cherish and honor the Dao, namely simply by constantly doing what is theirs to do.

The cosmology of the *Laozi* is based on the notion of *ziran*. The utmost efficacy (De) of the Dao that is at work in the cosmos and the ideal society is entirely self-generated[9] or *autopoietic*. This concept was coined by the biologists Humberto Maturna and Francisco Varela. It was later adopted by Niklas Luhmann for his new version of social systems theory. It is interesting to note in this context that there is in our time a concept of self-generation that, just as in Daoism, is used for describing natural and social processes alike. The expression "autopoiesis" is a neologism constituted by the ancient Greek words for "self" (*auto-*) and "production" or "generation *(-poiesis*). Niklas Luhmann explains how the word was "invented" by Maturana:

> Why autopoiesis? Maturana once told me how this expression came to his mind. Initially, he had worked with circular structures, with the concept of a circular reproduction of the cell. The word *circular* is a common one that does not create further terminological problems, but for Maturana it lacked precision. Then a philosopher, on the occasion of a dinner or some other social event, gave him a little private lecture on Aristotle. The philosopher explained to him the difference between *praxis* and *poiesis*. *Praxis* is an action that includes its purpose in itself as an action. Aristotle here meant the ethos of the life in the *polis*, its virtue and excellency, called *arête*, whose importance is not due to its contribution toward the creation of a good city; it rather already makes sense on its own. Other examples would be swimming—one does not do it in order to get somewhere—or smoking, chatting, or the reflections in universities, which too are actions satisfying as such without leading to any results. The very concept of *praxis* already

includes self-reference. *Poiesis* was explained to Maturana as something that produces something external to itself, namely a product. *Poiesis* also implies action; one acts, however, not because the action itself is fun or virtuous but because one wants to produce something. Maturana then found the bridge between the two concepts and spoke of *autopoiesis*, of a *poiesis* as its product—and he intentionally emphasized the notion of a product. *Autopraxis*, on the other hand, would be a pointless expression because it would only repeat what is already meant by *praxis*. No, what is meant here is a system that is its own product. The operation is the condition for the production of operations.[10]

This new—in Western natural and social sciences—concept combines the notions of productivity and absolute immanence. An autopoietic scenario is absolutely self-sustained, there is no external "input" or "output," but it is nevertheless a scenario of production—a scenario of continuous and unimpeded self-production and reproduction.

I do not know of any other concept in contemporary natural and social sciences that corresponds this well to the cosmological and social model of self-generation that we find in the *Laozi*. Of course, unlike in the highly complex theories of Maturana, Varela, and Luhmann, there is no systematic development of the concept of autopoiesis in the *Laozi*. There is, in a strict sense, no theory at all, and there is not even the explicit concept as such. However, if one wants to describe the model of cosmic and social self-generation that is so pervasive in the *Laozi* in contemporary terms, then I do not hesitate to call this model "autopoietic." While there is no *theory* of autopoiesis in the *Laozi*, the notions of *ziran, dao* and *de, yin* and *yang*, and *tian* and *qi* can, in conjunction, be read as elements of an archaic, prescientific, and pretheoretical model of autopoiesis.

As quoted above, in chapter 25 the Dao has only its "own course," its "self-so," as a rule. The cosmic process is rooted in itself. The Dao in the *Laozi* is not an origin, a principle, nor an ultimate beginning. It does not precede that which functions in accord with it. Neither the cosmos nor society has been "created" or "planned." Neither of them is grounded in some initial "action" or "agency." Neither the world of nature nor the world of man is "made." This is quite different from many cosmological and social theories that were influential in the Western tradition. Here we find a wide variety of "creators" and "makers," both in nature and among humans.

The Judean-Christian tradition has conceived of a creator God who was able to fabricate the world by his own powers and out of his own will. The Old Testament narrates the history of this "genesis" step by step, and it culminates with the creation of man "in the image of God." God, the creator, creates, as the crown of creation, creatures which are themselves creative. God had a plan and a will, and so do human beings. Even though not everything happens always as planned—not even necessarily as planned by God—the planner can always take measures, intervene in what is going on, or even modify his planning if he chooses to do so. In the *Laozi* we do not find such narratives of creation, planning, and management. The Dao does not create the world or manage it. And it does not invent a species of "assistant managers." Quite the opposite is the case: the Dao lets things happen "self-so," and if human beings want to succeed, then, according to the *Laozi*, they should try to follow its rather "non-creative" way.

In the Platonic version of a non-autopoietic creation, there is a so-called demiurge who acts as some sort of superior and initial craftsman—this is also what the word meant in the ancient Greek language. The demiurge is an artisan who makes things that were not there before. He has ideas in his mind and is able to shape materials accordingly so that they take on the form that he wants them to. In Heideggerian terminology, he is able to transform that which is "present-at-hand" (*vorhanden*) into that which is "ready-to-hand" (*zuhanden*). In the works of Aristotle, there is another version of non-autopoietic production and cosmology. Here, the universe and everything in it can be traced back to an "unmoved mover," the initial source of motion and change. In contrast to these ancient Greek and Judean-Christian models of creation and causation, the Daoist model avoids concepts of an original *act* of creation, of an entity that precedes its own creation, and an external source of energy. It has no preconceived goal "in mind," no ideas or plans according to which reality is shaped. Thus it has no intentions and no aim, it is non-teleological. The Dao is inseparable from its own productivity, it is totally immanent production—and so are human beings.

CHAPTER 4

Paradox Politics

The *Laozi* is certainly not a humanist text, and Daoist philosophy, in general, is not humanist either. Unlike for Protagoras, here man is not the measure of all things. Human beings are one element or segment of the functioning of the cosmos. Within this scenario, there is nothing special about humans. They were not created as the sole godlike species, are not the presumed master of the world, and are not even seen, in Heidegger's terms, as the "shepherd of being." Not only do humans lack the role of dominating nature or a special relation and responsibility toward "being," they are not even recognized as cognitively privileged beings, i.e., as *the* "rational animal." Therefore—and this may be somewhat surprising and perhaps even shocking to some Western readers—humans do not have a specific and unique "dignity." There are, consequently, no specific human rights. What is human is, in the *Laozi*, also "cosmic" or "natural." What can be said about humans can, more or less, also be said about other elements or segments within "heaven and earth"—and vice versa. The order and structure of human life is not different from the larger order and structure of the Dao. There is no particular form of existence, being, or *Dasein* to which humans have exclusive access and that is essentially denied to other beings.

The course of the Dao does not revolve around humans—it basically revolves around an *empty* center. Human life is then not at the center of attention in the *Laozi*. In this respect it certainly differs from many texts in the history of Western philosophy. Here, traditions as different as Christianity and Marxism, existentialism and rationalism, all came up with particular determinations of what it is to be human. In the Western tradition it is usually expected that a philosophical text has something distinct to say about the human being. The *Laozi*, I would say, should not be read with such an expectation since it will not meet it. There is hardly an attempt to single out or define the essence of man, and so, in the strict sense, there is not a genuine human "being" that is discernible from other beings. The *Laozi* takes no ontological approach and therefore does not try to answer the question of what "being" is for humans. The text is instead concerned with human behavior or functioning—and how this behavior or functioning can be optimized. An optimization of human functioning, however, is not different in structure from the optimization of functioning in general. In order to function well, humans are advised to function along with the Dao. Daoism is not humanism. It is, indeed, a *Dao*ism.

The non-humanist philosophical framework of the *Laozi* should not lead to the conclusion that humans and human life are unimportant issues in this text—the opposite is the case. While the non-humanism of the *Laozi* denies any privilege to the human species, and while there is nothing essentially human that the text is focused on, Daoism in general, and the *Laozi* in particular, is still *concerned about* human beings. Human society is seen as the most volatile and unstable segment in nature. Heaven and earth are normally "self-so" in order, but even in these realms there are occasional malfunctions and catastrophes. In human society there is an even higher propensity for such malfunctions (see chapter 23 in the *Laozi*). Unfortunately, man seems to be the greatest obstacle for the unimpeded working of the Dao. It is mainly for this reason that the *Laozi* talks about human issues. Consequently, it usually addresses all things human not so much in terms of "being," "essence," or "purpose," but with the exact same code with which it observes other things or segments of nature, namely order/disorder. Human problems in the *Laozi* (and quite generally in ancient Chinese philosophy) are mostly problems of order versus disorder, and thus are, in modern terminology, mostly "political" and "social." More specifically, the question asked is: how can order be sustained within the realm of human beings; and thus: how to govern humans effectively? Therefore, the *Laozi* did not aim at helping humans understand what they are, but at instructing a human ruler how to rule humans. It was not a text about humans, but a text about human leadership.

Insofar as the *Laozi* was a text about rulership, it was just as much a guidebook for political leaders as many other "philosophical" writings in China were at that point. The "disputers of the Dao" (to use A. C. Graham's way of speaking), i.e., the competing philosophical schools in ancient China at the times of the "Warring States" (*zhan guo*, fifth to late third century B.C.E.), typically disputed the best way of government while competing for access to rulers and influential advisory positions. There was a very strong political aspect to these philosophical discussions, and many sinologists—not only contemporary ones but also traditional Chinese scholars throughout the ages—have tried to reconstruct the meaning of these texts through aligning them with political opinions or factions.[1] As a guidebook on leadership and a manual for rulers the *Laozi* was, as pointed out above, initially meant to be "read" only by one person. The *Laozi* was a text for a very narrow social elite, it was not addressed to any "general readership." Such a notion, of course, would not have made sense in ancient China because most people could not read and there was no circulation of writings.

The quite exclusive distinction between possible readers and nonreaders is reflected in the actual distinctions between people in the text: its vision of order operates on the strict distinction between the ruler and the ruled. Order in the state is tied to this distinction as much as order in the body is tied to the distinction between the heart and the other organs. In the state, the ruler occupies the central position—which is solitary. He therefore relates to other people as the Dao relates to the ten thousand things. Through his singleness he provides for the unity of the political organism or mechanism. The distinction between the ruler and the ruled is a core feature of order that generates social cohesion. It is addressed in many passages in the *Laozi*. Chapter 2, for instance, says about the Daoist sage-ruler:

> *The ten thousand things—*
> > *he makes them work, but does not initiate them,*
> > *he makes them act, but does not depend on them,*
> > *he makes them complete their tasks and does not reside with them.*
>
> *Well,*
> > *only because he does not reside with them,*
> > *therefore they do not depart.*

This passage claims that the successful ruler "does not reside with" (*fu ju*) the ten thousand things, which can here be structurally equated with his subjects. The sage-ruler is the source of efficacy—but does not act. The ruler's position and function is diametrically opposed to those of all others, but this opposition is not antagonistic. It is, on the contrary, a functional necessity that unites the political and social organism or mechanics. The same chapter also states that "presence and non-presence produce each other," i.e., that fullness and emptiness have to come together to be productive and reproductive. In the state, the sage-ruler takes on the place of emptiness or non-presence while the people take on the place of fullness or presence.

The functional unity of the distinction between the ruler and the ruled is also highlighted in chapter 49. Here, their unity is described in bodily terms;

> *The sage is constantly without heart;*
> > *he takes the heart of the common people as the heart.*
>
> . . . .
>
> *When the sage resides in the world,*
> > *he fuses himself with it.*
> *For the world he merges hearts.*
> *All the people fix ears and eyes on him,*
> > *and the sage regards them as smiling children.*

The ideal ruler has no individual, personal heart—he is the heart of the people at the center of the community. His heart is empty of anything personal, he has no heart of his own, so that he can make room there for the hearts of all others. In this way he can fuse himself with the world. He unites the people into one political body but still remains different within this unity. All the people surround him and are directed toward him at the center, just as children turn toward their father and circulate around him. Only he remains in the solitary place at society's core.

The ruler's position is also different because he takes on the lowest of all positions. Following the strategies of reversal, as illustrated by the images of water and the feminine, he signals that he is "lying low" to express his supreme power and potential. In this way, he does not "pressure" the people from above but supports them from below. This is what chapter 66 of the *Laozi* says:

> *Exactly therefore:*
> *If the sage wishes to be above the people*
>   *he has to place himself below them in words.*
> *If he wishes to be at the front of the people*
>   *he has to put his person behind.*
>
> *Thus*
>   *when he is above the people,*
>   *they do not regard him as heavy;*
>   *when he is in front of the people,*
>   *they do not regard him as harmful.*

The ruler rules weightlessly, he is not a burden to the ruled. When he is "in front" of the people, he does not stand in their way and does not block or obstruct their actions. The sage-ruler in the *Laozi* has two characteristics: he is *inactive* and *without personal qualities*. The first aspect is expressed in the famous "doctrine" of non-action (*wu wei*), and the second in the important role of *wu* or non-presence. Chapter 48 explains how non-action results in ultimate power and is at the same time the key to holding on to it:

> *To decrease and to decrease even more;*
>> *so that "doing nothing"* [wu wei] *is reached.*
> *Doing nothing, and nothing is undone.*
>
> *If one wants to take hold of the world*
>> *one has to stay constantly without duty.*
> *As soon as one has a duty,*
>> *one in turn is not sufficient to take on the world.*

Only the ruler has no duties, no specific service to fulfill. If he would be of service, he would no longer be a ruler, but a servant. This would be like the hub trying to act like a spoke or water attempting to flow uphill. Chapter 64 says:

> *Those who act on things will be defeated by them.*
> *Those who take things in their hands, will lose them.*
> *Therefore the sage*
>> *will not act and thus not be defeated,*
>> *will not hold on and thus not lose.*

The same teaching can be found in chapter 29. Here, the advice for the ruler is again not to act and not to get involved in the business of "managing" things and events. This is left to others who perform their tasks "self-so" (*ziran*). The world or the state is compared with a "sacred vessel." It is hollow at the center and not for use.

> *If one wants to take hold of the world,*
>> *and act on it—*
> *I see that he will not succeed.*
> *Well,*
>> *the world is a sacred vessel,*
>> *and not something that can be acted on.*
> *Those who act on things will be defeated by them.*
> *Those who take things in their hands, will lose them.*

The non-action of the ruler is a recurring theme in the *Laozi*. It is often addressed, sometimes explicitly, sometimes implicitly. Chapter 43 speaks about the benefits of non-action and compares them with the benefits of non-speaking. Acting and speaking are parallel forms of behavior. The Daoist ruler remains silent because if he spoke he would have to say specific things and thus take on specific positions or opinions:

> *Therefore I know about*
> *the benefit of non-action.*
> *The teaching of non-speaking,*
> *the benefit of non-action:*
> *few in the world can get there.*

Non-action is the most important strategy for the ruler in the *Laozi*. In chapter 57 he is advised to identify with the following:

> *Therefore the words of the sage are:*
> *I do not act,*
> *and the people change by themselves.*
> *I love stillness,*
> *and the people correct themselves.*
> *I am without task,*
> *and the people prosper by themselves.*

The non-action of the ruler is connected to the "self-so" activity of the ruled. The distinction action/non-action is parallel to the distinction ruled/ruler. An aspect of the non-action of the ruler is his "hiddenness." He is as invisible as the root of a plant. Just as the root is always below the plant, he stays "under the surface" of the people. Chapter 58 begins:

> *Those whose rule is covered up and concealed—*
> *their people will be pure and sincere.*
> *Those whose rule is open and determinable—*
> *their people will be scheming and deceptive.*

The ruler certainly does not encourage people to "participate in government." He himself has no intentions to actively govern and no ambitions to steer the people in a particular direction—and the last thing he wants is to encourage the people to become political agents themselves. The ideal of government in the *Laozi* is certainly not "democratic." Even the ruler refrains from ruling and from forming a political will. One important function of his restraint is that it prevents his people from developing ambitions and the corresponding "political" means for getting their interests recognized at the cost of others. Once the political arena is opened, the scheming among the people will begin and they will use all sorts of cunning and deceitful behavior to gain power or influence. Presumably, the notion of an election campaign that many people today find to be an expression of a free society and a sign of good government would be quite abhorrent for a Daoist sage. This is not because he would be afraid of losing his powers but because such political activities would be a sign of a society in decay, a society in which people, rather than living their lives "simply," engage in cunning power struggles. The sage-ruler in the *Laozi* has no political desires whatsoever, and it is hoped that this will prevent such desires from arising in the state. If the ruler had an "agenda," or an "ideology," he would, willingly or not, most likely cause others to have different agendas or ideologies. If the ruler had no agenda and no ideology, then people would not enter political disputes and quarrels. There will be no political competition and strife—but not because such competition would be forbidden by a "totalitarian" regime. The ruler's main duty is to prevent himself, and subsequently others, from wanting to form a regime in the first place. To keep society peaceful and effective, the ruler has to ensure that order emerges from "nowhere" and that there is no observable person or personal interest at the center of power.

The Daoist ruler is qualified to hold political power because, paradoxically, he does not act politically and is not personally concerned with power and power struggles. Chapter 7 makes this quite clear:

> *Therefore the sage*
> *takes back his own person,*
> > *and will personally be in the front.*
> *keeps his own person out*
> > *and will personally be established.*

> *Is this not because he has no self-interest?*
> *Thus he can bring his self-interest to completion.*

The sage-ruler has no self-interest in ruling or politics. His only self-interest is to eliminate his selfish interest. Another aspect of the political abstinence of the ruler is depicted in chapter 22:

> *He does not make himself shown,*
> *and thus he is apparent.*
> *He does not make himself seen,*
> *and thus he shines.*
> *He does not acclaim himself,*
> *and thus he has success.*
> *He is not conceited,*
> *and thus he can last long.*

The sage-ruler's success and esteem is based on the absence of self-esteem. He is free of personal vanity and does not appear in public. His politics are not "populist" and he does not try to impress the people or strive for their sympathy. He is unconcerned with the impression people have of him, and so the people are unconcerned with him. He keeps their lives free of politics and thus keeps them out of trouble. Chapter 72 in the *Laozi* says:

> *Do not limit them in their dwellings.*
> *Do not oppress them in their livelihood.*
> *Well,*
> > *only if they are not oppressed,*
> > *will they not become weary.*

> *Therefore the sage*
> > *will master himself and not make himself seen,*
> > *will care for himself and not hold himself in esteem.*
> *Thus he rejects the one and takes the other.*

The sage-ruler holds himself in check. By holding himself back he not only prevents the people from being harmed by his politics, he also prevents himself from being harmed. He cannot be "burnt out" by his political life, there will be no stress for him in his office, because he does not act and does not compete. By not showing himself in public he not only keeps the public free of political worries, he also keeps himself intact as a ruler. His prestige never decreases because, paradoxically, it is not founded on any "colorful" qualities or obvious capabilities. There is nothing attractive in him, and people are not impressed by any of his traits. His prestige and political potency rather consists in his total lack of personal traits. Chapter 17 of the *Laozi* states rather famously: "Of the best of all rulers people will only know that he exists."

The "best of all rulers" is the least bothersome of all rulers. He does not allow for any "opposition" because there is nothing he stands for; there is no opposition against him because there is literally no "party" (no partial group) that is in power. Opposition is not oppressed; it cannot arise because there is nothing in particular to be opposed to. People who would want to "oppose" would have to take on specific opinions and express a desire to rule as opposed to others with other desires—they would be opposed to other people, but not to the ruler. By being opposed to other "parties," they themselves become a "party" and thus no longer qualify for being impartial rulers. The Daoist ruler is distinct from all others but opposed to no one. The central position is one of perfect neutrality, and to compete with it means to compete with that which does not compete. The absolute neutrality and impartiality of the sage-ruler means that one can neither oppose him nor side with him. Chapter 56 says:

> *Thus,*
> *one cannot get him and make him one's kin,*
>   *and one cannot get him and keep him distant.*
> *one cannot get him and let him profit,*
>   *and one cannot get him and do him harm.*
> *one cannot get him and hold him high,*

> *and one cannot get him and hold him low.*
> *Thus he is held high by the world.*

The ruler is not approachable, so no one can become his ally or his foe. Since he does not allow anybody to rally with or against him, no factional struggles arise. Since there are no factions, he enjoys the support of all. He maintains this univocal support by being nonpolitical, by governing without governing. Chapter 34 says about the Dao (of government):

> *The task is completed,*
> *the duty is fulfilled,*
> *but it is without name.*
> *The ten thousand things return to it,*
> *but it does not act as their ruler,*
> *so that it is constantly without desire.*
> *It can be named with the small.*
> *The ten thousand things return to it,*
> *but it does not act as their ruler.*

The nonpolitical ruler rules without ruling. Therefore he has "small" names. He is not glorified and does not take on grand titles that would designate him as a performer of great tasks. It is through the absence of names and tasks that he is given the greatest mandate, namely the "mandate of heaven." The Daoist ruler's mandate is to manifest the rule of the Dao within society. This mandate is not a mandate of or by the people, much less a mandate of or by some (or the majority) of the people. It is a mandate of "nature" that only the most impartial human being qualifies for. The mandate of heaven falls to the person who is able to totally "naturalize," and thus to totally "dehumanize," himself. The highest— and only—political mandate is not a mandate that emerges from a partial group, it is a mandate of a much broader range, and to take up such a mandate one has to be detached not only from specific personal interests but even from specifically human interests. The Daoist ruler's mandate is thus not a strictly political mandate, but rather a more comprehensive mandate within the larger context of "heaven and earth." After all, the political realm of human society is neither isolated from nor a privileged segment within nature. The Daoist ruler's mandate is to minimize human aspirations to overstep the human mandate, to minimize the "all-too-human" desire for active politics and literal government—in the sense of attempting to lead and steer things in a certain way. Any aspirations to impose a human rule over nature have to be prevented by the sage-ruler. Chapter 37 says:

> *The Dao is constantly without name.*
>   *If marquises and kings can maintain it*
>   *then the ten thousand things change by themselves.*
> *That which changes and then desires to take action—*
>   *I will subdue with the nameless, uncarved wood.*
>   *If it is subdued with the nameless, uncarved wood,*
>   *only then will it be blameless.*
> *By being blameless,*
>   *there will be tranquility.*

The rulers who rule in line with the Dao "subdue" the desires for power and political activity which will bring harm to society and nature by cultivating their own noncultivation, their nonhuman traits. They rule by being the "uncarved wood" that is not yet shaped into something particular, something useful for humans. The carved wood may fulfill a human purpose—but it no longer fulfills its natural function. The human ruler neither represents specific interests within human society nor any interests of human society that would oppose those of the "ten thousand things." The function of the political ruler of humanity is to prevent humanity from becoming self-interested. Rather than serving human interests, it is the ruler's function to prevent specifically human interests from developing in the first place. It is through this paradoxical form of governing that the ruler prevents human society from being blamed for disturbing the "tranquility" of the Dao.

According to Daoist mythology, such nonhuman and non-humanist rulers ruled in ancient times. They were shapeless and without names or titles, as chapter 15 says:

> *Of those in antiquity who were good at practicing the Dao:*
> *secret and subtle,*
> *dark and thorough,*
> *so deep as to be unfathomable.*
> *Well,*
> *just because they are unfathomable,*
> *one has to be forced to give a description of them.*

One cannot describe these ideal rulers of old in human terms—not because they were glorious "beyond" description, but because they did not have any specific traits. The imagery used in the above passage resonates again with the imagery of water and the female, the root and the valley. There are many poetic variations of the imagery of the shapeless and formless ruler. Perhaps the most intriguing "forced" description is found in chapter 20. The following passage from this chapter distinguishes once more between the ruler and the ruled. We witness a scene where the ruler actually appears among his people—in some sort of public ceremony, a ritual sacrifice or the annual official spring ceremony to welcome and initiate a new yearly cycle. The people are excited and exalted; the ruler, however, appears without an appearance. The people are highly active and in the light, but he remains, even in public, in the dark. Not only is he without action, but he is also without feeling or thought. He is a human "desert," an "idiot," an "infant that does not yet smile." He is the exact opposite of his subjects, but it is this opposition that will make the new year successful and fruitful. The ceremony seems to manifest the fact that the nonhuman ruler serves to "root" the activity of humanity in the greater functioning of the Dao. His non-presence in the midst of their presence guarantees that their ambitions are held in check, that their activities will not "autonomize" themselves. He represents the connection of the human realm to the cosmic realm of heaven and earth, the entrenchment of human activity within the greater context of nature, and confirms human abidance to the natural maxim of non-action. Chapter 20 says:

> *What desert! It never comes to an end!*
> *The ordinary people are in a good mood—*
> *   as if celebrating a great sacrifice*
> *   or climbing the terraces in the spring.*
> *I am serenely among them and do not show any sign,*
> *   like an infant that does not yet smile.*
>
> *What tiredness! As if there is no place to return to.*
> *The ordinary people all have in abundance—*
> *I alone have abandoned.*
> *I have the heart of an idiot.*
>
> *What simplicity!*
> *The ordinary people are shining—*
> *I alone seem to be hidden.*
> *The ordinary people are distinct—*
> *I alone am undifferentiated.*
>
> *What barrenness! It is like the ocean.*
> *What desert! As if it will never stop.*
> *The ordinary people all have their purposes—*
> *I alone am so stupid, to the degree of a yokel.*
>
> *My desires alone are different from those of the other people—*
> *   and I esteem the nurturing mother.*

The differences between the sage-ruler and the people are striking. He is formless and gives no signs, he is associated with endlessness and has no abode, he is empty—like the desert or ocean—and so is his mind. He is as stupid as a yokel. The people are "shining," they are distinct and have possessions and things to do. The contrasts are darkness/brightness, singleness/multiplicity, emptiness/fullness—the same that are found throughout the *Laozi*. Linguistically similar to chapter 20, but not referring directly to the sage-ruler, chapter 14 says:

> This is called:
>> shape without shape,
>> figure without thing
> This is called:
>> barrenness, desert

The same images occur in chapter 21, but here their paradoxical but immediate relation to fertility is highlighted:

> The thing Dao—only desert, only barren.
>
> What barrenness, what desert!
>> In their midst are the figures.
> What barrenness, what desert!
>> In their midst are the things.
>
> What nebulosity, what obscurity!
>> And what seminal energies in their midst!

Darkness and barrenness are the hidden sources of fertility, the pure potential of energy that nourishes everything. The Dao and the sage-ruler are identified with these non-qualities. The namelessness and shapelessness of the ruler align him with the Dao. By being associated with the desert and the barren, the ruler places himself where no one and nothing is or wants to be. This is the place from whence his efficacy emerges. Chapter 78 says:

> Therefore the words of the sage are:
> To take on the shameful in the state,
>> this is to be lord of the altars of earth and grain.
> To take on the unfavorable in the state,
>> this is to be king of the world.

The "shameful" and the "unfavorable" are those places in the dark and in the barren, places without name and form. By positioning himself there, and by identifying himself with their non-qualities, the ruler qualifies for being "the lord of the altars of earth and grain," i.e., the master of the ceremonies that unite human society and their agricultural production with heaven and earth, and thus with the cosmos or nature. It is only by the symbolical retreat to such "inhumane" locations that the ruler can serve his function as the connection between the humane and the non-humane. His radical retreat fulfills the double function of signaling that he is the only deserving regent as well as empowering him to connect society and the nonhuman cosmos. Such a position finally serves to provide the nameless and title-less ruler with some sort of designation—designations which are despised and avoided by everyone else. Chapter 42 of the *Laozi* says:

> *What the world hates,*
> *is to be orphaned, abandoned, and without possession*
> *and still kings and lords name therewith themselves.*

In fact, these were historical self-designations of the rulers. By calling themselves the "orphaned," the "abandoned," or the one "without possession," rulers symbolically located themselves in the "social desert." With these terms the rulers signaled their uniqueness as well as their alignment with the Dao—the shapeless and the barren. Through them, the rulers expressed their ultimate aloneness, their position in the midst of society, and difference from all others. They signaled that they lacked special relations with any group of humans and any specific function or role. That they had no specific family among humans, no father and son, made them the "son of heaven" (*tian zi*), which was another, more common designation for the regent. By being "orphaned" and "abandoned" among humans, the ruler signals that he is the mother and father of all—he has no specific relations and therefore is equally related to all. As with the Dao, his alone-ness paradoxically serves to establish all-one-ness, an all-one-ness that even includes "heaven and earth."

The *Laozi* develops an image of human beings and society as a cosmic sphere that is difficult to keep in harmony with the rest of nature. Human beings do not appear as "individuals," or "subjects," but rather as a sort of "social mass"—which can easily turn into a "social mess" if not ruled and ordered "wisely." Certainly, the *Laozi*, when it talks about politics, does not address philosophical issues such as the soul, free will, or human "dignity" that are so commonly involved in the discussion of human and social problems in Western traditions. Just like the other spheres in nature, the human sphere is, in the *Laozi*, a realm that can either be orderly and function efficiently or not. Human society is divided into sexes and duties, into different but correlative roles in family and in "production," but it is not divided into unique individuals. In order to make the social "mass" or organism function well, what is needed is not a sort of "consensus" among humans but an effective and harmonious arrangement of society, both internally and externally. The ruler has to fulfill, internally, the function of uniting all social functions into a single, unimpeded, and stabile process and, externally, to guarantee that this process is in line and in harmony with the processes of "heaven and earth." In order to be able to do this, the ruler cannot take on any specific task within human society. His leadership is built on being different from everyone else, and in particular, of having no "personality" of his own. If he was partial to any group of people, if he had a specific political agenda—if he was "political" in any way—he could not be the leader of all. He is the nonhuman center of human life. His main task is his "negative" self-cultivation. He has to dehumanize himself into an ego-less, shapeless being. If he succeeds, he will be able to be the pivot of human society, he will bring human activities into a perfect balance and rhythm. His leadership is, obviously, a leadership that does not lead.

The "paradox politics" of the *Laozi* are highly archaic and to some readers probably shockingly different from both modern and contemporary Western ideals of "enlightened" rulership. The humanist philosophies of the European enlightenment still dominate "our" understanding and self-description of politics and society. Common notions such as "democracy" and "human rights" symbolize the belief that government should be "by, for, and of the people," and politicians in the Western world usually pretend, at least implicitly, to be in line with such a "humanist" principle. It is generally believed that existing democratic states at least partially fulfill humanist ideals, and that they therefore represent progress toward a better and freer society—and that states or societies that have not yet made such progress would be well advised to undergo (or should be pushed toward) a "humanist" regime change.

Seen from a contemporary view, the democratic deficiencies of the political vision in the *Laozi* are obvious. The insistence on a single ruler who concentrates all political power in his position and, moreover, is very different from all others—so much so that he and his political "activities" remain completely hidden—may give rise to suspicions of a crude "totalitarianism" and may seem conspicuously close to the Legalist tyranny of the Qin dynasty. Certainly, the sage-ruler in the *Laozi* is not meant to represent the people or to be elected by them. Given the extreme historical and social differences between China in the second half of the first millennium B.C.E. and today's world, no one would seriously consider a Daoist ruler as a viable alternative in contemporary politics. Still, one may use the archaic model of paradox politics in the *Laozi* to critically challenge some currently dominant political beliefs. Since it does not share the humanist and democratic framework of the self-description of our society, the literally "outlandish" *Laozi* may allow for some uncommon perspectives on today's political "common sense" that otherwise often goes unquestioned.

One first question that may arise if one looks at present-day politics from the perspective of the *Laozi* is: Is a society that is so focused on human beings and their rights, such as individual freedom, personal property, and so forth, really and absolutely good? The *Laozi* would certainly provide room for criticizing the rather exclusively "human" focus of today's society in a somewhat similar fashion to the "deep ecology" movement.[2] In line with the *Laozi*, one may ask if "the people" should truly be considered the only authority and beneficiary of politics. The negative and highly destructive effects of "humanist" rule on the nonhuman environment are plainly clear. Still, it seems to be very difficult to implement a policy that would truly put the interests of, let's say, animals and plants, on par with the interests of humans. It is inconceivable how these forms of life could be given a political "voice" in a purely humanist and democratic society. They will never be able to vote, form a party, or put forth legislation. They are essentially excluded from humanist politics, and even the existence of a "Green" party cannot change this. After all, even Green Party membership is restricted to humans. The political view of the *Laozi* sees politics not so much as a tool for channeling human interests but as a mechanism that keeps human interests in check, and particularly, in line with the "interests" of "heaven and earth." The ruler in the *Laozi* is not so much a representative of his people as he is a "representative" of "heaven and earth" within society. His main function is to benefit society by including it harmoniously within the greater functioning of the Dao. It may be a political challenge to include such nonhuman interests in a "post-democratic" or "post-humanist" political theory.

But even if one were to accept the idea that politics and social power should be exclusively given to "the people," one could ask from the perspective of the *Laozi*: Why are only the people who live in the present given power—what about future human beings? Or, why are many who live in the present excluded from voting because of citizenship, age, a criminal record, and so on—don't these people also count as humans? So the final question could be: Is a so-called democratic society actually able to be what it pretends to be, namely a "rule by the people"? Why does a group of people of a certain age in a certain country have the privilege to make political decisions that have an effect on those who cannot take part in the process (foreigners, children, inmates, etc.)? Isn't voting always "biased" in the sense that people put their own interests above others? From the perspective of the *Laozi*, political rule should ideally be perfectly unbiased and impartial—the ruler keeps his distance from society to preserve his absolute neutrality. The ruler is "father and mother" to all—and not just a particular "party." Just as a "post-democratic" and "post-humanist" political theory might try to integrate political mechanisms that would broaden the source of political authority beyond the human realm, it may also try to work toward forms of rulership that strive toward higher degrees of impartiality among those who have political power. Such mechanisms, for sure, are already in place, for instance through nonelected courts and nonelected international assemblies. From the perspective of the *Laozi* it would make sense to counterbalance biased elected centers of power with inherently less partial political institutions. According to the *Laozi*, ultimate political power should rest within an institution that is totally free of any bias or subjective interest. It is questionable if such an institution is really possible, but it might make sense to work toward the creation of institutions that come closer to this ideal than governments that are elected by the interests of a necessarily selective group of people.

Third, the rule of the Daoist sage in the *Laozi* is clearly based on the principle of non-agency. This is also in stark contrast to the self-description of political rulership in a humanist society. Here, through freely forming a government, the people are supposed to really "steer" (this is the etymological root of the verb "to govern") themselves, to take their fate in their own hands, to manage the world. Such an "activist" conception of politics is alien to the *Laozi*. It rather believes that a paradoxical type of management is most effective—a management in which the CEO, so to speak, mostly does nothing. Given the dominating "activist" agenda of politics and management, such a strategy may seem, once more, "outlandish." Still, if one takes a closer look, it is not that far from reality. Contrary to the self-description of the current political system, it is actually not clear if, for example, a president can do much about the economy or other social developments. Does the president of a country really steer what goes on economically, legally, or educationally within the country? It seems that social developments, most obviously in the economy, are not under the control of governments but, to a large extent, systemic processes. Maybe the "national" rulers are already much more Daoist than they think they are. If so, then why not try to amend the dominating self-description of contemporary politics and include a Daoist element that would acknowledge that leaders often do not—and cannot—lead?

CHAPTER 5

On War

From politics it is not far to war. As Carl von Clausewitz famously remarked, war can be understood as the continuation of politics by other means, and this insight is certainly not incompatible with how the *Laozi* conceives of the interrelation between these two social phenomena.[1] Throughout most of history, reflections on politics and war have been tightly interwoven, and thus a political philosophy is quite naturally related to a philosophy of war. In the *Laozi*, this relation is both obvious and close. In the preceding chapter, I attempted to point out how the *Laozi* looks at politics as both an important element within the general order of the cosmos and a rather troublesome source of all kinds of problems. Politics is a very delicate issue to deal with and a difficult matter to handle successfully—so difficult, indeed, that it needs a sage. Politics cause problems, in the view of the *Laozi*, because it is "all-too-human," and only Daoist sages are able to "dehumanize" politics—by their own self-dehumanization they minimize the potential for human and social malfunctions. The political sage in the *Laozi* takes a non-humanist approach to resolve or, more precisely, prevent social crises and conflicts. War—as the continuation of politics by other means—can well be defined as the worst-case scenario of such political crises and conflicts, and if the sage's function is to prevent political crises, then this implies, perhaps most importantly, the prevention of war. In this way, the sage's main political role or "goal" in the *Laozi* may be defined as the establishing of peace, and this is sought by "dehumanization."

Many studies point out that, historically, ancient Chinese philosophy flourished in the period of the so-called "Warring States" and that recognizing this context is crucial for correctly grasping the philosophical issues at stake. This is also true with respect to the *Laozi*. It was a guidebook for political leaders in times of more or less continuous war, and therefore the topic of war is not only treated theoretically but also practically. The political ruler to whom the *Laozi* is addressed was at the same time (at least potentially) a military leader. Political and military strategy are thus inseparable in this text, and they are both paradoxical: The best way to achieve social and political stability is not to be politically active; and the best way to deal with war is to prevent it from happening in the first place. But when war cannot or could not be avoided, the best way to restore peace is to win smoothly and swiftly. These are the two main concerns of the *Laozi* in regard to war and its strategy: preventing it or ending it successfully.

If, as in the *Laozi*, war is a political problem and a case of social disease, an "inflammation of the state," so to speak, then its causes will be similar to those of other social defects. War can thus be understood as the most extreme symptom of general social or political disorder. As shown in the preceding chapter, political disorder is an effect of uncontrolled human strife. War is, in other words, a harmful eruption of desires. The immediate relation between war and human desires has been noted by many philosophers, Chinese and Western, ancient and modern, alike, and is quite obvious. While other philosophers, such as Hegel, for instance, conceive of this relation as a necessary moment of human existence, the *Laozi* hopes that a sage-ruler will be able to minimize, if not totally eliminate, harmful and excessive desires, and thus achieve political calm. In the *Laozi*, the minimization of human desires is the key to social harmony. The process of minimizing human desires has to be initiated by the sage-ruler. Then, it is believed, peacefulness will spread among the people. If the sage-ruler succeeds in simplifying and dehumanizing himself, then the people will follow his example. Chapter 57 of the *Laozi* ends with the saying:

> *I desire without desire,*
> *and the people turn to simplicity by themselves.*

If the sage-ruler reduces his own political desires—desires for power, wealth, possessions, and so on, then this will determine the political "climate" of the state. The people will not develop such desires and there will be a general "mastery of satisfaction" (*zhi zu*), or "mastery of cessation" (*zhi zhi*)—to use expressions that occur in the text itself (in chapters 32, 33, 44, 46). The self-restraint of the ruler causes a self-restraint in society, but the *Laozi* also describes the opposite effect. Chapter 46 explains in detail what will happen if the rulers are unable to restrain their own and thus their subjects' desires:

> *Of the crimes none is greater*
> *than to allow for desires.*
> *Of the disasters none is greater*
> *than not to master satisfaction.*
> *Of the calamities none is sadder*
> *than the desire to acquire.*

In the *Laozi*, the things in the world most closely associated with desires and most immediately attached to their fulfillment are weapons. War is the concrete political situation that manifests the material connection between desires, weapons, human emotions, and a decaying society. Weapons create desires by creating the possibility of fulfilling them—at the expense of other people. War, itself an expression of human desire, stirs human desire. War is human desire in action. Ancient Daoist philosophy shudders at such an intensity of desires, and at the social disorder and the heightened activity that comes with it and is so clearly destructive. Daoist anti-activism is particularly concerned with aggressive and violent action. To the *Laozi*, any "voluntary" action is suspicious and potentially dangerous, and war is, here, the very worst type of human activism. While not being entirely "pacifist"—and thus certainly different from some forms of

Christian opposition to war—the *Laozi* nevertheless repeatedly, and in an uncommon clarity for this otherwise notoriously "obscure" text, voices a deep contempt of warfare. Chapter 31 says:

> *Weapons are not the tools of the noble man.*
> *Weapons are the tools of ill omen.*
> *When he cannot do otherwise, he uses them—*
> > *to him staying calm is the best.*
> *Do not regard them with delight.*
> *To regard them with delight—*
> > *this is to enjoy the killing of men.*
> *Well, by enjoying the killing of men*
> > *one is unable get what one wants in the world.*
>
> . . . .
>
> *Therefore*
> > *the lieutenant general stands to the left*
> > *and the supreme commander stands to the right.*
> *That is to say:*
> > *they are positioned in accordance with funeral rites.*
>
> *When masses of people are killed,*
> > *this is faced with grief and sorrow.*
> *When a war is won,*
> > *the occasion is treated with funeral rites.*

The *Laozi* finds nothing attractive in war and weapons. To have a liking for weapons means to have a liking for killing men—a liking for slaughter. Such likings will prove to be socially disastrous, and a man with such likings is not fit to be a ruler. Weapons cannot be separated from their function, they are the technology of aggressive action and violent desire. The sage-ruler does not like them and refuses to make use of them if at all possible. But in the event of war, the Daoist sage will do so without positive emotions. The sage will not fight enthusiastically but will remain perfectly calm. There will be no frenzy of warfare, and there will not even be triumph in victory. A war is a symptom of failed policy and thus before battle the sage-ruler's army is already positioned in accordance with the funeral rites. After the battle the sage-ruler does not indulge in feelings of "satisfaction," there were no desires to be filled. All that remains are the dead and, if this gives rise to any emotions, they will be of sorrow and grief.

The main function of weapons in the Daoist society is to deter or prevent war. In typical Daoist fashion, they function best paradoxically. They fulfill their purpose if they are unused—only thus do they lose nothing of their efficacy, stay intact, and do no harm. Chapter 80 in the *Laozi* states:

> *Let there be a militia and weapons,*
> *but people do not use them.*

The military is needed, but not to be employed; and if it has to be employed it has already failed to some extent and is doomed to lose some of its efficacy. Even in the case of victory, it is hard to avoid damage. An army that is used will suffer casualties—it is a truism that war is always costly, even if fought successfully.

The military and the weapons of the state serve to deter and prevent war, and they have to be hidden away so that they will not arouse the desire to use them. A military parade is not something a Daoist sage-ruler would approve of. If weapons are shown to the people they might begin to feel strong—in the double sense of this expression. Chapter 36 of the *Laozi* advises the sage-ruler:

> *Fish are not to be taken out of the depths.*
> *Sharp tools are not to be exposed to the people.*

Displaying weapons is believed to be dangerous because this may actually entice people to use them. The political power of the Daoist sages is tied to their being "in the dark," and the same is true for their military power. To them, to expose oneself politically is to arouse political desires, and to expose oneself militarily is to arouse aggression.

If, however, a war develops, the Daoist sage will turn into a military commander who can win the war by adhering to the paradoxical strategies of the *Laozi*. Just as the elimination of desires is the best way to avoid war, it is also the best way to win it. The enemy will be defeated by defensive tactics, by holding one's own ambitions and desires in check. The military's aim is to exhaust the enemy through making him act, while the Daoist commander avoids aggressive actions himself.[2] The enemy, taking the initiative, will be made to constantly invest energy and force and will thus finally tire out. The enemy will suffer defeat from overextending his resources. Chapter 68 describes these tactics that are still an integral part of East Asian martial arts:

> *Those who are good warriors*
> *are not belligerent.*
> *Those who are good at battling*
> *do not get angry.*
> *Those who defeat their enemies*
> *do not engage them.*

The martial arts of the *Laozi* are founded on passivity and defense. Daoist warriors stay hidden and do not display themselves, they avoid direct friction and contact. War is a game of power in which, ultimately, the side that squanders its powers will lose. As in politics, a leader has to focus on continuously preserving one's full efficacy by not exposing oneself. By practicing utmost restraint one does not become emotionally involved or stirred. The leader avoids anything that could give rise to vulnerability. The art of war consists in making the enemy defeat itself by an overexpenditure of energy. The Daoist commander wins by mastering the "efficacy of not fighting" (*bu zheng zhi de*), as chapter 68 of the *Laozi* puts it. Chapter 69 conveys the same message in somewhat more detail:

> *With respect to the usage of weapons there is a saying :*
> *"I do not dare to be the lord,*
> *and rather be the host.*
> *I do not dare to go an inch forward,*
> *and rather retreat a foot."*

> *This means:*
>
> *taking steps without taking steps;*
> *rolling up the sleeves without baring the arms;*
> *taking hold without the force of weapons;*
> *defying without engaging the enemy.*

The first line of chapter 69 indicates that its subsequent lines are a "saying," and this means, as Robert G. Henricks remarks in the notes to his translation of the chapter, that it was probably a proverbial expression associated with the contemporary school of the "Strategists" or "Militarists" (*bing jia*).[3] Similarly, Roger T. Ames and David Hall point out in their translation that the message of these and other verses in the *Laozi* "resonates closely with the *Sunzi* tradition"[4] (the *Sunzi* being probably the most important "strategical" or "militarist" text in ancient China). Thus, the military strategy advocated in the *Laozi* can well be understood as a "mainstream" position. Within the larger context of ancient Chinese reflections on warfare, it does not present a unique Daoist perspective. Instead, it represents a view that seems to have been rather generally held at that time and was in line with the then dominating "semantics" of war. The following short anecdote is found in the *Zuozhuan*, an ancient Chinese historical compendium that has no specific Daoist tendency but nevertheless illustrates well the "efficacy of not fighting." Here, the story is about a man named Cao Gui, who accompanied the Duke of Lu as a military adviser in a battle against the state of Qi. The *Zuozhuan* says:

> When the duke was about to beat the drums [to let his army attack], Cao Gui said: "It can't be done yet." When the men of Qi had beaten their drums three times, Cao Gui said: "Now it can be done," and the army of Qi was defeated. . . . [Later] the duke asked [Cao Gui] for the reason why [he initially hadn't allowed for the drums to be beaten]. Cao Gui said: "Well, war is a matter of courage. When you beat the drums once, the courage is stirred. When you beat them again, the courage declines. When you beat them a third time, it expires. Their courage expired while ours rose. Therefore we overcame them."[5]

The army of Qi lost the battle because its strength had expired before it was even used. The military version of the Daoist maxim of "doing nothing and nothing is undone" (*wei wu wei er wu bu wei*) was obviously held in high regard among ancient Chinese military strategists—but even in Western history it is not too difficult to find evidence for its practical value. Günter Wohlfart has observed—and rightly so, I believe—that one of the greatest military "upsets" in Europe was brought about by the implicit application of Daoist tactics: Napoleon's expedition into Russia was utterly defeated by the constant nonengagement of the troops of the Czar.[6] The total destruction of the "Grand Army" was not achieved on the battlefield but precisely through the avoidance of aggressive combat by the Russians. In his endless pursuit of the always evasive enemy and in "conquering" the deserted city of Moscow, Napoleon completely exhausted his military and suffered a devastating loss. Most of his soldiers were not killed in battle but, rather, by cold, starvation, and social disintegration. Napoleon simply miscalculated the forces of "heaven and earth," he was not defeated by "manpower" but by "nature."

Despite this rather impressive example of the potential efficacy of a military tactics in line with Daoist and, by extension, ancient Chinese stratagems, the semantics of "nonengaging" warfare did not enjoy such popularity in Western traditions. Often, the "iconography" of war in the Western tradition differs significantly from that of war in the *Laozi*. As opposed to many Western images of war and warfare, the "defensive" *Laozi* does not connect war with heroism, justice, and collective pride.

Since Greek antiquity, Western representations of war have been tightly connected to images of heroes and deeds of heroism—and this general trend continues uninterrupted into the Hollywood movies of today. Of course, there is a wide range of different forms and types of heroes and heroism, and it is difficult to subsume all these under a single denominator, but in stark contrast to the significance of the "icon" of the hero in the Western history of war, the *Laozi*, although very much concerned with matters of war, lacks such images. In the *Laozi*, the military leader appears, if seen from the perspective of heroism, more like a coward. He is, if at all possible, on the retreat; he shuns battle, and his major concern is to stay hidden as much as he can. He clearly does not rely on "shock and awe." Another kind of warrior that one does not find in the *Laozi* is that of the "lethal weapon" type—to use the title of a popular series of American movies. The "lethal weapon" character has gone through some sort of personal experience that has hardened him into a "desperado." His despair, his lack of hope in his personal life, has turned him into a fearless, risk-taking fighter. His fearlessness, however, gives him an aura of invincibility. He thus becomes a master fighter—because he has no fear, he is feared by others. This type of warrior is typically a loner, a unique individual with a strong "subjectivity." The "lethal weapon" character serves as a Western model of what it can mean to be a warrior; and an army of such warriors would consequently be an assembly of very special people, a collection of unusual men. The *Laozi*, however, is not interested in the individual psyche of the soldiers. There is no focus on the subjective qualities of war. It is seen as a social or group phenomenon rather than something decided by extraordinary personalities. Even—or rather, particularly——the highest military commander lacks a unique personality. He has to restrict all his personal issues and desires; his individual "background" is of no relevance or, rather, he has no background, psychological depth, or complexity.

A figure related to the lone warrior is the passionate fighter, a Gen. George S. Patton type, a man whose whole (masculine) emotionality is focused on war and triumph in battle. He is the soldier who is literally in love with war—and more in love with it than with anything else. Similar characters can be found in modern Western literature, for instance in the novels—and autobiographical writings—of Ernest Hemingway. Again, there is nothing like this in the *Laozi*; the element of passion and (male) ecstasy is practically absent from its depiction of war—or at least from war successfully fought.

In comparison with the above patterns of heroism, the military leader in the *Laozi* is clearly an antihero, he lacks all their "glorious" qualities. From the perspective of the *Laozi*, however, this lack is, of course, the very condition for his success—and seen from this angle, the Western hero appears more like a fool, a person who is doomed to end tragically by becoming a victim of his own activity and strength. The genre of tragedy is highly respected in Western literature, and it is closely related to the Western iconography of war and heroism. This is, once more, in striking contrast to ancient Chinese culture in general, and to the *Laozi* and Daoism in particular. The *Laozi* was interested in how to be effective, and not in glorious failure. In fact, it had difficulty in seeing any glory in failure at all.

In addition to having strong individual qualities, typical Western war heroes are also normally moral agents. More often than not, the fights they fight are just. Interestingly enough, this moral dimension of warfare is also practically absent from the *Laozi*. The world of war in this text is not divided into "good guys" and "bad guys," but in winners and losers. In fact, there is no "just cause," no "good reason" to go to war in the *Laozi*. As stated above, here war can well be understood, in line with von Clausewitz, as a continuation of politics by other means, but basically as a continuation of *failed* politics. The Daoist general does not fight a war out of moral necessity, he does not try to impose a good political agenda on an evil opponent—he has no moral or political agenda at all. The *Laozi* does not speak of "punitive" wars, it does not bring anybody "to justice." And neither is there a semantics of war as a liberating effort—neither of self-liberation nor of the liberation of others. In the *Laozi* none of these moral and political agendas and semantics can "justify" or "necessitate" war. The *Laozi* does not make any rhetorical attempts to adorn warfare at all. In this text, war is primarily seen as a social disaster and, consequently, there are two very simple and practical attitudes that it advises. First: avoid it. Second, if you cannot avoid it, win it with the least possible damage to yourself. Neither of these attitudes is in need of moral glorification. In fact, from the perspective of the *Laozi*, talk of a "just," a "necessary," or a "liberating" war can, like heroism, appear as the somewhat presumptuous and pompous self-aggrandizement of a social loser.

As a social disaster, war in the *Laozi* is also not a matter of collective pride. The Western iconography or semantics of war, particularly in modern times, is connected with collective sentiments such as feelings of national identity and honor. Modern Western nations could publicly define themselves by the wars they fought, a nation could claim to be "born" in a war. A war is, even today, often celebrated as a national effort. Here a people can show the world, and, maybe more importantly, itself, its supposedly "true character." War and nationalist frenzy have often been not far apart in the history of the modern Western nation-state. The military that fights for a nation identifies itself with its "father-" or "motherland" and, vice versa, the whole nation, in "supporting our troops," develops a "culture" of national identity. Again, such a national dimension—a dimension of collective pride—is totally absent from the discussion of warfare in the *Laozi*. While, in the modern nation-state, war often serves as a means for bringing about political stability and unification—in wartimes the "nation" can be expected to rally around the government and the army that it commands—such a function is absent from early Daoism. The Daoist leader keeps a "low profile," and particularly so in war. From this perspective war shames a government rather than giving the people reason to love their leaders and country. A war is not a sign of political resolve and mass identity but of social divisions, political disharmony, and disunity. The *Laozi* does not cherish social conflict and therefore has no vocabulary for celebrating war as a time that can define a people.

The differences between a Western war "heroics" and the strategic philosophy of war in the *Laozi* are quite substantial, and they may be just another aspect of the difference between humanist and non-humanist "ideologies." The *Laozi* does not view war as a specifically human event—it is not won by individual fighters nor by charismatic leaders, and it has no power to define specific groups. It lacks all human grandeur. It is rather described and analyzed as a political malfunction that, unfortunately, occurs rather frequently, just like some natural disasters. It is up to the sage-ruler to deal with war as effectively as possible and, if unable to prevent it, to restrict the harm it does. War, like politics, is a social phenomenon that operates not on the basis of humanist principles but within the context of a larger nature and cosmos. The strategies of dealing successfully with it are not different from the strategies for success in other areas. These strategies are variations of the non-humanist maxim of "doing nothing and nothing is undone."

Humanist semantics, on the other hand, associates war with human achievement and with individual and collective growth. Of course, a humanist perspective on war can also be critical of war and develop in a pacifist direction. War can also be condemned on humanist grounds, it can be denounced out of compassion and commiseration for human individuals. But even this perspective is absent from the *Laozi*. The *Laozi* does not "on principle" take a stance against war, it is not seen as a "crime" against humanity or as a sin. Perhaps pacifism and heroism are, in the humanist semantics of war, as closely related as Dr. Jekyll and Mr. Hide—and, consequently, neither of them appears in the *Laozi*.

CHAPTER

Masters of Satisfaction

(DESIRES, EMOTIONS, AND ADDICTIONS)

Human desires are identified as a main cause of war and social disorder in the *Laozi*. They are at the core of the "human problem," i.e., the problem of achieving the same degree of natural functionality among humans as within "heaven and earth." The personal cultivation of the sage-rulers is thus focused on minimizing desires and corresponding emotions. It is believed that if they succeed in eliminating harmful desires in themselves, this will not only grant them great social prestige but also influence their subjects. If there are no desires at its "heart," the whole social body will be without desires. It will be internally and externally peaceful. The sage-ruler's heart at the center of the community *is* at the same time the "empty" heart of all (see chapter 49). The sage-rulers are not the "face" of the state, they do not "democratically" represent the people but, quite to the contrary, the character of the state mirrors their achievements in self-cultivation. If they cultivate restraint, their community will likewise. But if the rulers are desiring despots, their rule will result in a desiring and despotic society. War as a state of social crisis will inevitably result from desiring rulers and a desiring state.

The "peacefulness" of the Daoist sage-ruler is an effect of a total eradication of personal ambitions. The rule of the state is nothing that the sage literally "wants." The sage-ruler's lack of political ambition is—unlike the case of the ideal philosopher-king in Plato's *Republic*—less a result of a certain reluctance to get involved in the "dirty" business of politics but, rather, one (important) aspect of the general lack of *any* wants or desires. The sage-rulers have no desire to rule because they have no desires whatsoever. The ideal rulers in the *Laozi* neither like nor dislike ruling—since they have no likes or dislikes to begin with. They are not only socially but also emotionally without bias.

The emotionally "cool" Daoist sage-ruler is quite different from the Confucian model of a good regent or a good human being in general. Confucianism emphasizes the shaping of adequate and harmonious human feelings. In a sense, the whole Confucian "project" can be described as one of cultivating human emotions. It is famously stated in the Confucian *Analects* (1.2)[1] that "filial piety" (*xiao*) is the "root" (*ben*) of "humaneness" (*ren*)—the latter being something like the "cardinal virtue" of Confucianism. "Filial piety" is of critical importance in Confucianism because all human development depends on it. Here the metaphor of the root is used slightly differently from the Daoist version but is no less illustrative: the whole social and emotional life of human beings is literally "rooted" in their childhood experience and upbringing. If a child does not learn from early on how to feel and behave "correctly," then its biological, psychological, and social foundation is not properly grounded. The general Confucian belief is that through developing the appropriate feelings of love and respect toward one's parents—and *only* thus, in a society like ancient China where the family was the core social unit—a human being grows into a "humane" person. That one, later in life, will be able to naturally feel and behave correctly in all social situations depends, from the Confucian perspective, on one's ability to develop the correct feeling toward one's immediate social "peers" in the earliest years. Throughout the course of one's life, emotional training never ends. The function of ritual—the rules of proper behavior—is to provide society with pervasive ceremonial structures not only for special occasions but for practically any event in everyday life. Ritual propriety will allow everybody to not only act adequately but, at the same time and equally important, to have the *adequate emotions.* Funeral rites, for instance, serve not only to provide people with guidelines for what to do when a loved one has passed away but also, and again at least equally important, to provide one with the appropriate *feelings*. The Confucians are ancient "behaviorists," they believed that in behaving a certain way one would have the corresponding feelings. Human beings who have cultivated their "filial piety" will "naturally" grieve their deceased parents with the adequate intensity and in the appropriate way. The funeral rites are the behavioral complement to the emotional state in such a situation. Emotions and rites together channel feelings and actions and harmonize them with those of all others in society. Emotional and behavioral cultivation are inseparable in Confucianism and are the two aspects of a society that interacts harmoniously. They not only channel individual feelings and actions but organize the emotional and behavioral life of the whole human community.

As opposed to the Confucian attempt to train and channel emotions and behavior through ritual—concretely, for instance through ceremonies of grief (e.g., funerals) and joy (e.g., seasonal festivities)—so that they will result in appropriate behavior and social cohesion, the *Laozi* tends to advocate an emotional "fasting." While the "root" of filial piety symbolizes the solid and healthy beginning of what is perceived to be a process of growth in Confucianism, the root image in the *Laozi* is more associated with qualities of invisibility, shapelessness, darkness, and being unmoved. Both usages of the image are equally "natural," but while the Confucians focus more on the developmental aspect, the *Laozi* highlights "noninterference." The root serves the plant well, according to the *Laozi*, because it does not intend to "be in the light." The root lets the plant grow by staying hidden itself. The self-restriction of the root allows the plant to grow and wither unimpeded—it is "disinterested" and does not evoke any desires in the plant. The Daoist root functions like an anchor that, without active force, keeps the ship from going astray. Or in other words: the "root" image in Daoism is not so much a symbol of "human" development as an illustration of the unmoving center within a biological cycle.

The root metaphor in Confucius' *Analects* is associated with the cultivation of feelings; in the *Laozi* it is associated with the absence of emotional excitement. Many passages in the *Laozi* poetically describe the "disinterested" Daoist sage-rulers. Chapter 39, for instance, says:

> *For this reason they do not desire*
> *to be shining like jade,*
> *to be hard like stone.*

Politically, the "desirelessness" of the sage means that only those who are without personal desires are qualified to be rulers; they are, so to speak, the "natural choice." At the same time, it is exactly this quality that enables the leader to stay in power and rule successfully. If the seductions of power take hold of a leader, and if he develops desires along with his superior position, he will ultimately lose it. Before he loses power, he will, most likely, have brought his country into crisis. A ruler who develops desires will tend to exploit his state, to take from his people, and to start a process of political and even economic decay. He thus turns from being a follower of the way (*dao*) into a "robber" (also pronounced *dao*, but written with a different character) of his own people. This will, in turn, produce a society in which people have to become robbers themselves to survive. Chapter 53 in the *Laozi* depicts the sad state of a country of "robbers" by highlighting the stark contrasts that arise there between, on the one hand, the desolate general situation and, on the other, the decadent lifestyle of the corrupt regime. It gives a rather drastic description of a "politics of desire:"

> *The court is very neglected.*
> *The fields are very fallow.*
> *The granaries are very empty.*
>
> *The clothing is ornamented and colorful,*
>   *there is a sharp sword on the girdle.*
> *Satiated with food,*
>   *there are more than enough goods and possessions.*
>
> *This is called: "Robbery."*
> *Robbery is not the Dao.*

Such circumstances are not unheard of even today. A government that is mainly focused on fulfilling its own desires will tend to neglect its administrative duties and be more concerned with increasing its wealth and power. It will indulge in luxuries while the people are starving, it will expose its weapons—the rulers carry their sharp swords—and be prone to using military force, both internally and externally, to protect its possessions.

The *Laozi* supposes that the effect of such "politics of desire" are not only economic and social but also "psychological." When the heart of the social body is infected by desires, the rest of society will also naturally become infected. If the sage-rulers want to avoid such social conflict, they have to prevent the arising of desires in the first place. Thus chapter 3 in the *Laozi* gives the following advice:

> *When the goods that are difficult to obtain are not esteemed,*
> *then this will make the people not become robbers.*
> *When that which is desirable is not displayed,*
> *then this will make the people not disorderly.*
>
> *Therefore the ordering of the sage is such:*
> *He empties their hearts;*
> *he fills their bellies.*
> *He weakens their wishes;*
> *he strengthens their bones.*

The sage-ruler rules "negatively" and diminishes the demand by not exposing the supply. If the supply is not publicly exposed, desires are kept in check. Obviously, the *Laozi* did not envision a capitalist market economy with its culture of creating demand and desires through advertising and a public ideal of ever-increasing prosperity. The early Daoists, it seems, were not interested in "heating up" the economy by stimulating the acquiring of goods and possessions. Consumption was meant to remain rather basic. The ruler would fill people's bellies by emptying their minds; they would feel satiated with what they had as long as their desires for getting more were not stirred. In this way, people's bodies would be healthy while their minds remained undisturbed.

The Daoist elimination of desires is thus paradoxically grounded in their fulfillment. Desires are prevented from developing by bringing about a basic and general state of satiation. Once one has eaten, it is argued, one will "naturally" have eliminated one's desire to eat. One eliminates one's desire to eat simply by eating; one eats in order to not desire to eat anymore. Desires only arise if one does not eat to be satiated. Or, in other words, the elimination of desire is the result of the "mastery of satisfaction" (*zhi zu*), or the "mastery of cessation" (*zhi zhi*; see chapters 32, 33, 44, 46). The Daoist sages are "masters of satisfaction" because they know when to stop. Not knowing when to stop means, quite logically, never to be satisfied. The very emergence of desire is thus a symptom of failure in the mastery of satisfaction. Only those who are not satisfied desire. The sage-rulers aim at bringing about general satisfaction—not only for themselves but for the states they rule.

The Daoist sages' mastery of satisfaction allows them to be persons of great taste. They have a rare and refined sensibility and thus become very specific gourmets. Since they are free of desires they have no specific craving for "extreme" tastes. Thus they are able to taste what most people cannot—and here, once more, they are like infants, they are not yet attracted by spices. Their taste is so sensitive that they can eat and taste the tasteless. That which is without any taste is, as chapter 35 in the *Laozi* says, the Dao itself. And chapter 63 suggests:

> *Taste the tasteless.*

The Dao is not only empty and shapeless, it also without any specific taste. In order to be able to taste the tasteless, one has to overcome—or to reduce—individual sensual preferences. By being inclined to specific tastes, one will inevitably harm one's sensual capabilities. This is the topic of chapter 12, which, among similar verses, says:

> *The five tastes*
> *make a man's palate obtuse.*

It is quite natural that people who like to eat, for instance, hot or sweet meals will, over time, desire to eat even hotter or sweeter dishes. Once used to a certain level of hotness or sweetness, the earlier level is no longer sufficient. This leads not only to an increase in desires but also to an increasing dissatisfaction with most of what there is to eat. The hotter one has to eat to be able to taste the hotness of the food, the less is one able to taste hotness. Those of whom we usually say are good at eating hot foods are actually the opposite: they are not good at the tasting of hot because they need a lot of spices before they can even begin to appreciate the hotness of their dishes. In this way the taste for hotness actually destroys the taste for hotness. This development of desires is not "evil," it is just not very efficient. It ruins the taste. It becomes harder and harder to be satisfied, and the range of what is satisfying gets smaller and smaller.

If one loses the taste for the tasteless, one is already on the path to desire and thus less and less a "master of satisfaction." Such a person destroys, so to speak "the sixth sense" for that which does not have any taste at all. When this taste is lost, satisfaction is hard to get. The most efficient gourmet is the one whose taste is rooted in the perseverance of the supremacy of the taste of the tasteless. This supremacy consists in the fact that the tasteless is the only taste that never loses its intensity and does not take anything away from tasting other tastes. By tasting the tasteless, one does not create a need for something that is even more tasteless, nor does it harm the perception of other tastes.

Sensual desires are not attacked in the *Laozi* as evil lusts or human deficiencies. It does not aim at denigrating the pleasurable but, paradoxically, at optimizing pleasure. The *Laozi* tries to develop a "logic" of the interrelations between desire, satisfaction, and taste. Desires indicate the absence of satisfaction, and satisfaction indicates the absence of desire. In order to reach the second state and to avoid the first, it is suggested that one be sparing with one's tastes. If one develops a taste for intensity, one will unavoidably harm one's initial capacity of taste.

In other words, the Daoist attitude toward desire that is found in the *Laozi* is not ascetic, it does not advocate a forced denial of pleasures. It does not attempt to "purge" oneself from bodily pleasures or "sinfulness." As mentioned above, desires are not "evil"; they are not ethically but "medically" rejected: they are symptoms of discontent and therefore not "good." Instead of being ascetic, the *Laozi* rather advocates a paradoxical hedonism that aims at achieving perfect contentment in one's present situation by preventing the emergence of (ultimately insatiable) cravings that would necessarily "relativize" one's present and natural contentment. In contemporary language, one could say that it aims at preventing addiction—if addiction is understood as a state of compulsory consumption that never leads to actual fulfillment, a self-perpetuating state of desire that continuously projects satisfaction into the future. The *Laozi* wants "immediate" and present satisfaction, and it argues that such immediate satisfaction is only possible if no desires exist that violate a perfect contentment with the present. Desire, in the sense of addiction is, from the perspective of the *Laozi*, always a state of discontent because it presupposes that true satisfaction is possible only in the near future.

The *Laozi* does not clearly differentiate between states of the body, the mind, and society, and its attempt to eliminate addictive desires refers to all three realms. The contentment it speaks of is clearly bodily—that bellies have to be filled is certainly meant literally. Also the five senses are, of course, immediately related to bodily functions. The state of the body is, however, inseparable from mental or emotional states. If one is in a state of bodily contentment, then it is assumed that one's emotions will likewise be at rest; and if one is in a state of bodily desires, then one is also mentally dissatisfied. Physical and mental states are, in turn, also conceived of as being immediately manifested in social states. A society based on desire—as, for instance, a capitalist economy—is from this perspective inevitably a society of *general* addiction. The non-humanist *Laozi* does not really distinguish between the state of "individual" beings and their community. Society does not consist of singular personalities but is, so to speak, a social organism. If this organism is "bodily" and "mentally" geared toward desires and addiction, then this is at the same time a social phenomenon. Addiction is not an "individual" defect—it is a general state that has physical, psychic, and social dimensions. The "project" of preventing addiction and establishing satisfaction is therefore as much a medical project as a social project. From the philosophical perspective of the *Laozi*, one could say, to use the above example again, that addiction and an economy based on the continuous creation of demand are parallel phenomena. It is not that one phenomenon is the "root cause" of the other; they are rather two contingent but correlative types of a state of desire—in the double meaning of the word *state*.

Desires, as the *Laozi* sees it, do not spoil our souls or our innocence, but they spoil our tastes, our contentment, and, ultimately, our social harmony. The desires that the *Laozi* is concerned with are not even principally "bodily" desires: as is explained in the second chapter of the present volume, early Daoism is not prudish. A nonphysical desire that can be socially harmful (and potentially more harmful than sexual desires) is the desire for knowledge. This intellectual desire is also mentioned in the third chapter in the *Laozi*, from which I quoted above. In order to prevent the emergence of unhealthy emotions and intentions among one's subjects, the Daoist sage-ruler is advised in the following way:

> Persistently he makes the people have no knowledge and no desires.

Even the urge to know or to know more has to be prevented. The "information society" is certainly not something the early Daoists had in mind for their ideal state. A capitalist economy focused on permanent demand and a media system focused on constantly providing new information open up new types of compulsions. Once we are used to getting our specific dose of information renewed every day—the news, the soap opera, the sports results—another addiction is established. In a capitalist and information society, we are not only continuously in a state of possessing money but, at the same time—and this does not even change for the rich—of having not enough. Likewise, by having a lot of knowledge we also lack knowledge. Even after hearing today's news, we do not know, for instance, what will happen tomorrow. As the German sociologist Niklas Luhmann puts it: "Fresh money and new information are two central motives of modern social dynamics."[2] The "hunger" for information functions parallel to the hunger for money, and, as opposed to the hunger for food and for sex, the former two hungers are not essential for reproduction. This illustrates once more the nonmoral Daoist attitude toward desires. Desires are, strictly speaking, unproductive addictions, and therefore they are problematic. Sexual desire and the desire to eat only become problematic when they prevent one from having "good" sex and satisfying meals. Otherwise, sex and eating cannot even be called desires—having "good" sex or a satiating meal is, from a Daoist perspective, the elimination of a desire. Desires for possessions and information are more problematic because there is no form of ultimate satisfaction to be reached in these activities, they have no inbuilt mechanism that allows for moments of pure present contentment. In sex we can have an orgasm, when eating we can be full. This is not difficult. But is there truly an orgasm in wealth, and when is one satiated with knowledge?

The less knowledge one has, the less potential one has for desires. Knowledge too can make people unhappy and irritate them. It can contribute to being dissatisfied with the plain and simple. Knowledge can stir up emotions and produce mental states that may cause social disorder. Next to desires, knowledge can endanger social harmony, and thus many chapters in the *Laozi* (for instance, chapters 10, 47, 48, 65, and 81) argue against it. Desires, knowledge, and the inventions and techniques which result from applied knowledge are, from the perspective of the *Laozi*, prone to cause emotional trouble. At least, this is what chapter 57 says:

> *If the people have many sharp tools,*
> *the state and the families will increasingly be in disorder.*
> *If men have a lot of knowledge and sophistication,*
> *there will increasingly appear weird things.*

Knowledge and emotions do not make people happier, because they cause trouble and make things more difficult to deal with. Emotional and intellectual efforts produce "stress" and lead to a loss of energy and harmony. Emotions and knowledge can harm social cohesion and obstruct the realization of an important Daoist goal, i.e., the establishment of a permanent order. An investment into emotions and desires may well be an investment into one's downfall. This is expressed in chapter 44 with a laconic sentence:

> *Where there is deep sympathy,*
> *there is great expenditure.*

The expenditure of feelings is certainly not seen "romantically" in the *Laozi*. Instead, it is blamed as a violation of the principle of simplicity and calmness. Nature is not exciting and not excited and, from the Daoist point of view, avoids states of agitation—it does not even fall in love. And when, in some exceptional cases, nature is stirred—for instance when there are whirlwinds and rainstorms (see chapter 23 in the *Laozi*)—this signals that something is wrong. For humans who are eager to include themselves seamlessly into the "Dao of heaven and earth," it is therefore important to cultivate emotional calm. The person who excels most in this cultivation is best suited for becoming the regent. The Daoist sage is the least emotional and desiring person in the state.

CHAPTER 7

Indifference & Negative Ethics

The twentieth-century Chinese-American writer Lin Yutang retells the ancient Chinese story about "the old man at the fort" (which is found in the text *Huainanzi*) in the following way:

> There was an old man at a frontier fort in the north who understood Daoism. One day he lost his horse, which wandered into the land of the Hu tribesmen. His neighbors came to condole with him and the man said, "How do you know that this is bad luck?"
>
> After a few months, the horse returned with some fine horses of the Hu breed, and the people congratulated him. The old man said, "How do you know that this is good luck?"
>
> He then became very prosperous with so many horses. The son one day broke his leg riding, and all the people came to condole with him again. The old man said, "How do you know that this is bad luck?"
>
> One day the Hu tribesmen invaded the frontier fort. All the young men fought with arrows to defend it, and nine tenths of them were killed. Because the son was a cripple, both father and son escaped unharmed.
>
> Therefore, good luck changes into bad, and bad luck changes into good. It cannot be known where their altering ends.[1]

The *Huainanzi* is a textual compilation ascribed to Liu An (178–122 B.C.E. ?) that contains many more or less Daoist materials. The above story, particularly in light of its last two sentences, can be understood as an illustration of a short passage in chapter 58 of the *Laozi*:

> *It is upon bad luck*
> *that good luck depends.*
> *It is upon good luck*
> *that bad luck depends.*
> *Who knows where it ends?*

The old man at the fort was obviously in a state of emotional calm. Good luck did not make him happy and bad luck did not make him sad. He was *indifferent* to both. His emotional indifference or equanimity, however, does not mean that he was unable to differentiate between having a horse and not having one, but he did not know which was essentially better. There was then no reason to be either depressed by one or exalted by the other. Having horses and not having them are not the same, they are different—they are as different as night and day—but it is exactly their difference which makes them elements of a course of change. If they were the same, there would not be a change from one to the other.

As opposed to some rather simplistic prejudices about Daoist philosophy and that of the *Laozi* in particular, it does *not* deny differences. The emotional indifference of the Daoist sage, or of the old man at the fort, does not mean he is unable to differentiate. The emotional indifference of the Daoist sage results, for instance, not from being unable to differentiate between the having and the not-having of horses, but from conceiving of this difference not as one between good and bad. To him, there is no ultimate good luck or bad luck. Events turn into each other—like night and day, like growth and withering. None of these events constitutes an "end."

The indifference or equanimity in the face of good and back luck acknowledges the equal validity of two necessary events or stages. They equally contribute to a cycle of change, and it would be terribly one-sided to attach one's feelings to one stage at the expense of the other.

The emotional indifference of the old man at the fort goes along with his claim to not know rather than know. He is not only emotionally indifferent but also indifferently ignorant. He does not know that what is called good will be ultimately good or that what is called bad will be forever so. His ignorance and his equanimity go together, and they result from restrained judgment. The acceptance of change means that there is no partiality. The Daoist sage knows that things change, and because things change there is no telling of what is good and bad.

Emotional states are tied to such knowledge claims. In order to be sad about something, one has to believe that one knows that that which one is sad about is thoroughly bad—and the same is of course the case with being happy about something good. To minimize one's emotions and to approach indifference is therefore intrinsically related to the minimization of knowledge claims. In a quite Socratic fashion, the old man at the fort and the Daoist sage know that they do not know; and this is the reason why they are wiser than those who pretend that they know, but who, because of this, are truly ignorant.

The emotional equanimity and minimization of knowledge claims allows the Daoist sage to affirm that which is present without *ressentiment*. The old man at the fort does not suffer from his bad luck and does not rejoice in his good luck. He is, so to speak, without Buddhist suffering and Christian joy. The old man at the fort can live through his bad luck without suffering from it, and through his good luck without feeling blessed or "saved." The equanimity of the Daoist sage is not a spiritual elation or salvation, there is no soteriology attached to it. The sage is obviously not entirely free from bad luck. The harm of bad luck is, however, minimized. If one is able to minimize one's emotionality and intellectual tendency to evaluate, one is no longer subject to the emotional and intellectual friction caused by unfortunate circumstances.

Chapter 58 in the *Laozi* as well as the story of the old man at the fort illustrate the absence of a one-sided attachment or identification with either favorable or adverse circumstances. They do not simply say that all wounds will heal or that some good always comes out of something bad. They are not meant to be emotionally soothing or comforting. This would just be another form of emotional "care" or investment, and a one-sided one too. Wounds do tend to heal, but people also become sick, and there is usually some bad that results from good things as well. There is no escape or overcoming of bad luck. But according to chapter 58 of the *Laozi* and the story of the old man at the fort, neither good nor bad luck are "substantial." They are segments of a process of change.

The alternation of good and bad luck is an important issue in ancient Chinese philosophy. It may well be said that Chinese philosophy originated, at least partly, from the practice of divination. The oldest layers of the *Yijing* or the *Book of Changes* are oracular formulae, and the entire book is concerned with the complementarities of situations of good and back luck—not so different in content, but much more "obscure" in style, from the story of the old man at the fort. The notions of good luck (*ji* or *fu*) and bad luck (*xiong* or *huo*), along with the related notions of order (*zhi*) and disorder (*luan*) as well as the rhythm of Yin and Yang, were, so to speak, the basic code of ancient Chinese philosophy, and they also figure prominently in ancient Daoism and in the *Laozi*. Their alternation is related to the philosophy of change, which is also a topos that connects the *Yijing* and the *Laozi*.

A short line—or should one say a *catchphrase?*—in chapter 40 summarizes the philosophy of change in the *Laozi*:

> *Reversal is the movement of the Dao.*

The course of the Dao is one of reversal, situations turn around and change into their opposites. This can be said with respect to good and bad luck, but also to night and day, Yin and Yang, and so forth. Daoist sages are able to respond to the course of change with indifference: they are able to equally accept the opposing segments or phases of the movement of the Dao without being one-sidedly attached to a singular element. The sage has no partiality. The emotional indifference of the sage corresponds to the ability to indifferently accept the different as different, but at the same time as equally valid and necessary segments of the course of the Dao.

There is a relatively long passage in chapter 2 of the *Laozi* which lists a number of complementary segments of change or opposites:

> *Everybody in the world knows the beautiful as being beautiful.*
> *Thus there is already ugliness.*
> *Everybody knows what is good.*
> *Thus there is that which is not good.*
>
> *That*
> > *presence and non-presence generate each other,*
> > *difficult and easy complement each other,*
> > *long and short give each other shape,*
> > *above and below fill each other,*
> > *tones and voices harmonize with each other,*
> > *before and after follow each other*
> *is constant.*

The complementary segments listed in this chapter are not only complementary "categories" like good and bad or beautiful and ugly; they are also, and maybe even primarily, phases of change. The linguistic "frame" of the six "pairs" in the second "stanza" states that these pairs are "constant." The nonconstancy of the segments constitutes a constancy of change. When, for instance, a wheel turns, when what is above turns into that which is below and vice versa, the two "fill each other." Tones and voices in a musical performance constitute a harmony not only synchronically but, and perhaps more importantly, diachronically. A musical performance is a temporal sequence of tones. Long and short are moments of a process of growth. Before and after are obviously the constituents of time.

In the course of time these segments change into each other and, once more, this change is only possible because the segments are different. The sage's indifference toward them does not mean that they are "all the same," but that the sage is able to equally appreciate them as equal components of a "movement of the Dao."

If one reads the second stanza in this way, one may conclude that the same "message" is also contained in the first stanza. The beautiful and the ugly, the good and the bad can also be temporal: beautiful people can become ugly over time and, again in connection with the story of the old man at the fort, what is good can turn into what is bad, and vice versa. The sage is able to differentiate between beautiful and ugly, between good and bad—everybody can do this. But unlike everybody else, the sage is able to be emotionally indifferent and impartial toward both opposites. These lines in chapter 2 of the *Laozi* are ironical: Everybody "knows" that the beautiful is beautiful and that the ugly is ugly, that the good is good and that the bad is bad. But only the Daoist sage, like the old man at the fort, does not know that one of the segments is better or more valid than the other. As opposed to others, only sages are able to equally appreciate the two moments as equally constitutive of reality or of the movement of the Dao. They are, once more, not prejudiced against either the ugly or the bad. To them, the ugly is ugly and the bad is bad, but this does not bother them because they understand that these are mutually dependent elements of change.

There is another chapter in the *Laozi* that contains a series of opposites, and again, these opposites seem to be understood as being not only complementary but also temporally sequential. Chapter 22 says:

> *Flexed then whole,*
> *bent then upright,*
> *hollow then full,*
> *worn out then new,*
> *little then gaining,*
> *a lot then confused.*

After a plant is "worn out" in the winter it grows anew in the spring. In the beginning it is small, but it continuously grows larger; when one shoots a bow it is first bent and then upright, when one uses a container it is first hollow and then full, and so on.

The impartiality and equanimity of the sage translates quite seamlessly into the political neutrality of the sage-ruler. The sage-rulers unite the opposites not by negating their differences but by showing no preferences. Thus they can provide the "oneness" that is needed to integrate the opposites into a continuous and harmonious whole.

Another even more obviously social type of opposite is addressed in chapter 20 of the *Laozi*:

> To agree politely and to reject angrily—
> how far are they apart from each other?
> To find something beautiful and to find something ugly—
> in which way are these apart from each other?

In social interaction people communicate with each other approvingly or disapprovingly—these are the two "poles" of talking to another. Of course they are different, but the two attitudes constitute the frame of social exchange. So, while they are certainly different from each other, they are not entirely separate. They are the necessary opposites that make it possible for language to *proceed*, for talk to go on. Similarly, to approve of something as "beautiful" and to dismiss something as "ugly" are certainly two completely opposed judgments, but, again, it is only through their opposition that judgmental activity as such becomes possible. While being different, the two pairs of opposites can well be understood as being mutually dependent. From the perspective of the sage, each of the two different communicational attitudes—acceptance and rejection—are equally important for communication to take place and to continue.

The Daoist sage's neutrality and indifference with respect to opposites such as long/short, before/after, or above/below will not seem strange to many readers. Even the equanimity in regard to distinctions such as beautiful/ugly, good luck/bad luck, or agreeing/rejecting will probably seem plausible while viewing them within the Daoist philosophical context. We are quite willing, for instance, to "emancipate" the ugly and admit that it may also have its merits. We do not necessarily always value a model more than her certainly less attractive, but perhaps wiser, grandmother. The sage's indifference, however, becomes problematic in regard to the moral distinction between good/bad or, to put it in more religious terms, the difference between good and evil. But even if this may seem somewhat scandalous, I would argue that, from a Daoist perspective, indifference is particularly important when it comes to moral evaluations. The sage in the

Laozi is also morally impartial or, in Nietzschean terms, beyond good and evil. Chapter 49 says the following about the Daoist sage:

> That which is good
>   he holds to be good.
> That which is not good
>   he also holds to be good.
> Thus he attains goodness.
>
> That which is true
>   he holds to be true.
> That which is not true
>   he also holds to be true.
> Thus he attains truth.

The Daoist sage does not take sides in moral quarrels or in quarrels about what is right or what is wrong, about what is true and what is false. Just like the old man at the fort, he does not ultimately know what is good or bad and what is right or wrong. The story in the *Huainanzi* particularly illustrates, at least as I read it, this amoral morale: Moral distinctions are as much prone to reversal as any other distinction. There are no final judgments possible in moral discussion and therefore it is wiser to refrain from making them. Actions that seem to be good may well have bad consequences, and actions that seem to be bad may well have good consequences. What is taken to be true today turns out to be false tomorrow, and what is seen as false today becomes right tomorrow. In any case, both evaluations are interdependent. Both are equally part of a reality that comprises both stances. To isolate one side at the expense of the other means to be unable to "get the whole picture."

The sage's indifference in moral issues is all the more important because morality is so volatile. Moral differences may easily turn into conflicts, and these often lead not only to quarrels but to the use of force and violence, if not to war. Moral distinctions are potentially dangerous. In nonhuman nature there is no morality to be observed. Winter is not more "evil" than summer, it is just colder. In the human realm, however,

INDIFFERENCE AND NEGATIVE ETHICS

moral distinctions can easily turn antagonistic. Thus, a complementary distinction can become adversarial. Morality thus poses a major threat to social stability. If the sage-rulers would be partial, they would violate the balance in society and become antagonistic themselves. Therefore they refrain from moral judgments. By not taking part in moral communication and communication about right and wrong, the rulers prevent these communications from turning violent. Their neutrality prevents a partisan struggle. Chapter 22 says about the sage-ruler:

> *Well,*
> *it is because only he does not struggle*
> *that nobody can struggle with him.*

And chapter 8 states similarly:

> *Well,*
> *it is because only he does not struggle*
> *that there are no calamities.*

The same chapter also says:

> *The best is like water.*
> *The goodness of water consists in*
> *its being beneficial to the ten thousand things,*
> *and in that it, when there is contention, takes on the place*
> *which the mass of the people detest.*

The sage is the only one who does not takes sides. All others, the mass of the people, tend to identify with certain positions—they say, for example, that good luck is good and bad luck is bad. The noncontentious sage is the only one who remains indifferent and thus prevents the difference from becoming a contentious social division.

The noncontentious indifference of the sages with respect to moral distinctions makes them quite different from the ideal Confucian rulers. And this is famously or, from a Confucian perspective, notoriously, expressed in chapters 18 and 19 in the *Laozi*. Here it sharply condemns the virtues that the Confucians expect from a political leader. Chapter 18 says:

> *When the great Dao is dispensed with,*
> *then there is humanity and righteousness.*
> *When knowledge and smartness come out,*
> *then there is great falsity.*

The Daoist ruler does not aspire to humanity (*ren*), righteousness (*yi*), wisdom or knowledge (*zhi*). This is in stark contrast to Confucian "orthodoxy" and must have been truly scandalous in the context of ancient Chinese philosophy where these virtues were "normally" highly cherished. Is the Daoist sage-ruler an immoral autocrat? Does his emotional and moral indifference amount to total heartlessness? Is he blind to human suffering? I guess the answer to these questions is both yes and no.

Probably the best-known philosophical defense of the above-mentioned Confucian cardinal virtues was brought forth by Mencius (371–289 B.C.E. ?). For Mencius, humanity, righteousness, and wisdom constitute, along with ritual propriety (*li*), the "four germs" (*si duan*) of human character, the inborn dispositions (*xing*)[2] common to all human beings. To justify this claim about the "four germs," he constructs the following example:

> Suppose a man were, all of a sudden, to see a young child on the verge of falling into a well. He would certainly be moved to compassion, not because he wanted to get in the good graces of the parents, nor because he wished to win the praise of his fellow villagers or friends, nor yet because he disliked the cry of the child. . . . Man has these four germs just as he has four limbs.[3]

Menicus argues that the Confucian virtues are derived from inborn qualities, that they develop from a kind of "moral sentiment," to put it in modern Western terminology. These "germs" are then believed to be the reason why people will, without hesitation, help a child that is about to fall into a well. Does the *Laozi*, then, given its suggestion to abolish the "four germs," deny these sentiments, and does it implicitly say that a Daoist sage would not come to the rescue of a child in danger? Here, I think, the answer is no.

An immediate "Daoist" response to the example given by Mencius may in fact be, in connection with the story about the old man at the fort, that one cannot ultimately know that the rescue of the child will be good at all. Maybe the child will become a mass murderer later in life, maybe it is a little Adolf Hitler who is about to drown, and so one can never know if rescuing the child will actually be beneficial. Or one might argue, from a somewhat extreme Daoist-Darwinist point of view, that children who are so clumsy that they fall into wells do not really contribute to the genetic development of the human race. Helping them would not be in the interest of nature. Still, I do not believe that either of these responses is truly in the spirit of the *Laozi*. I think that the Daoist sage, as introduced in the *Laozi*, would rescue the child, but I would still maintain that this would not be done for "moral" reasons—and that the sage would do it *indifferently*.

In my view, a "truly" Daoist philosophical response to the example given by Mencius is the following: The *Laozi* would say, I believe, that we do not need the "four germs" to rescue a child whom we see drowning. We would do so not because of morality, but because it is simply natural. The *Laozi* is quite clear in saying that the "four germs" are not among the qualities of a Daoist sage—but the *Laozi* would also claim that none of these "germs" is inborn in the first place. What the *Laozi* seems to say is that, as opposed to the Confucian assumption, moral virtues are not only not inborn, neither are they necessarily good. According to the *Laozi*, we may conclude, there is no need to develop a *virtue* that would have us help a child in danger. Instead, the *Laozi* would claim that it is a *natural impulse* to help a child in that situation—even a dog would react in such a way if its puppies were about to be harmed. There is no obvious need for qualifying such a natural reaction as *morally good*. Yes, everybody would save the child, but from the perspective of the *Laozi*, it does not make sense to call this act "good" as opposed to "bad." The Confucians' mistake is the labeling of such an act as "morally good" instead of just natural or instinctive. We also do not ascribe morality to animals that protect their offspring. Why is one then forced to declare something which is merely natural and instinctive as "good" or "bad" and thereby establish an evaluative and artificial distinction that will probably give rise to social trouble, namely, the distinction between good and evil deeds and thus good and evil people. For the *Laozi*, there is no particular merit in claiming that one's natural instincts are somehow morally superior.

The Daoist sage would therefore help the child without emotion or a feeling of moral elation. A sage would not even expect praise for helping the child and would not want to be called "good." Instead, the sage would be very suspicious of the celebration of such natural acts as good, because through such celebrations of morality one in fact creates, however unintentionally, divisions in society. By singling out a person or a group as good, one automatically devalues others as being not as good. Morality is, from a Daoist perspective, not so much an inborn quality that leads to good deeds, but a form of communication that creates divisions and may lead to disputes or social antagonisms.

Morality can be dangerous, it can easily become a social pathology.[4] One may not only develop an undue amount of arrogance and individual self-appreciation, but, collectively, a highly "moral" society will be prone to view others as less moral and less worthy and therefore, perhaps, as enemies. It is not by coincidence that moral language and moral self-praise is especially popular in times of war and conflict. The Daoist ethics is negative. It does not assume that moral evaluations or even that moral sentiments are necessary to do good. If one only acts "indifferently," one is already able to act well. There is no need to engage in a potentially harmful moral discourse.

CHAPTER 8

Permanence & Eternity

The indifference of the Daoist sage relates to the acceptance and affirmation of change. To be indifferent means to equally appreciate different, but complementary, segments of a process of change. It is believed that only the indifference to the different guarantees the smoothness of change and thus its unimpeded continuity. Therefore, the Daoist philosophy of indifference and change is also connected to a philosophy of time—a philosophy that turns out to be one of permanence rather than eternity.

Permanence is one of the great topics of Daoism, and it is of particular importance in the *Laozi*. Its many images of vegetation and fertility (such as the root, water, the valley and the river, the female) demonstrate that Daoist permanence is closely related to the permanence of natural processes or "cycles" of production and reproduction. Nature "happens" as a permanent process of production. This is most obvious in regard to the four seasons, which are a basic pattern of regulation in an agrarian society. The permanent course of the four seasons orders human activity and labor. The regular return of the seasons, the renewed growth of life in spring, is a cornerstone of human and cosmic survival—the permanence of the productive course of time is fundamental for sustaining both nature and culture.

The "new birth" of life in the course of time—for instance, the blossoming of flowers and trees in springtime—is not entirely a *new* birth; it is rather the seamless continuation of a process of reproduction, and of life and death, which is never essentially interrupted. The course of the seasons corresponds to the course of the heavenly bodies in the sky. Day and night change in a regular fashion—and every "new" day is new by itself, but also a continuation of the always ongoing process of change from darkness to brightness.

Just as day and night change within "heaven and earth," so do phases of human activity and rest. Similarly, summer and winter represent such phases when not only nature but also society is more or less active. Time, like Yin and Yang, is rhythmic. Rhythmic time is orderly, and the order of time leads to its continuity. What is continuous is so because of its inherent orderliness. Time in nature is orderly and continuous, and it is up to humans to take part in this structure of time. If they are able to do so, they will follow the "way"—or the Dao—of time.

Nature, however, does not only show patterns of regularity, it also shows examples of momentary interruptions. From time to time the order is disturbed. Sometimes what is supposed to live long dies young, or something that is supposed to grow does not. Sometimes it does not rain when it is time, or it does not get warm when it should. Sometimes natural disasters and catastrophes occur, like, for instance, floods and droughts. The permanent course of time is always in danger—there is always the fear of a sudden break. Chapter 23 of the *Laozi* describes how the productivity of natural process can turn into destruction:

> *A whirlwind does not last a morning.*
> *A downpour does not last a day.*
> *Who is acting in these cases?*
> *Heaven and earth—*
> *but even these can't make them last.*

In the case of the whirlwind and the downpour, time has lost its regularity—non-lasting events have intruded into the course of permanence. The regular order of time and weather has been violated, and the result is disaster and the untimely killing of life. The harvest may be spoiled, the crop may be destroyed. Instead of orderliness, there is an untimely disruption. This is the other side of permanence. When the order of time is violated, this affects not only time but "heaven and earth" and, thus, human society. Such events mark the intrusion of untimeliness into the temporal order.

In nature, the exchange between heaven and earth is one of a rhythmic giving and taking. If that giving and taking functions properly, then there will be perpetual reproduction. But when the rhythm is interrupted, reproduction comes to a halt. It is of utmost importance to prevent these interruptions and to keep the rhythm of time ongoing. If humans do not follow the natural rhythm, they may well lose what they need to survive. If even the heavenly bodies and the earth, those most stable functionings in the world, are in constant danger of losing their constancy, then this danger looms all the more over human society. "Heavenly" time is quite naturally in order, but the same cannot be said of human time. In the political realm, as well as in the "cosmic" cycle of the year, it is of the utmost importance that everything happens at the right time. If people do not sow and harvest at the appropriate time, or if administrative orders are issued in an untimely way, there will be a social crisis.

In ancient China the ruler had to ritually open the seasons, particularly the season of spring when the new agricultural cycle began. Even more important, the ruler or the government had to establish the calendar. Astronomy was therefore crucial. The most critical function of the calendar and astronomy was not the mere quantitative measuring of time, but rather the correct administration of time. The government had to supervise the timeliness of human activities. By establishing the calendar, society was able to follow nature and thus to assist nature in its continuity. The calendar enabled society to act in accordance with the rhythm of heaven and earth, and it was the ruler's duty to oversee the calendar's appropriateness and to partake in the timely activities that it prescribed.

The sage-rulers not only had to regulate all agricultural work with the help of the calendar, they had also to pick the right time for "sacred" events, such as the sacrificial ceremonies, or for more common activities—such as going to war. Thus chapter 8 of the *Laozi* says about the Daoist sage-ruler:

> *In having actions performed,*
> *His goodness lies in timeliness.*

It is the ruler's responsibility to perform the offerings for heaven and earth at the correct time. In administering public services he has to be careful not to interrupt agricultural production, and in war everything depends on attacking or retreating at the right time. Failing to do any of these activities at the proper moment may well lead to the downfall of a state.

Timeliness also implies that once a thing's time has passed, it must pass on. In order not to obstruct the course of time, events have to make room or, rather literally, to "make time" for the events that are to follow. Chapter 44 in the *Laozi* explains this:

> *To know when it is enough is to be without disgrace.*
> *To master cessation is to be without peril.*
> *Long duration becomes possible.*

Permanence is not only dependent on events not coming too early but also on events not staying too long. "Long duration" only becomes possible when all the segments of the permanent process neither miss nor exceed their appropriate time. A season that goes on too long obstructs the arrival of the next. An activity that takes longer than it should prevents the timely beginning of the following event. In this way, the order of time is violated. "Too long" is as dangerous as "too short." This is obviously the message of these lines in chapter 64:

> *Therefore it is said:*
> *Be as careful with respect to the end as with respect to the beginning,*
> *then you will not suffer defeat in your undertakings.*

When the segments of time are connected in a continuous chain, the end of one segment marks the beginning of another. Thus, beginning and end are interdependent and equally important moments for temporal continuity. They are both crucial divisions within the course of time. If one is "good" in "timeliness," then one will have to be as considerate to the end as one is to the beginning. Just because the course of time is not supposed to end, specific phases have to end when their time is up. Permanence depends on the "mastery of cessation" (*zhi zhi*).

The *Laozi*'s conception of time as permanence is established on the basis of the distinction permanence/interruption. Permanence is the perfect form of time, and it is realized when there are no interruptions. Uninterrupted permanence, however, is not the permanence of the same, but rather the permanent and seamless change from one segment of time to the next. Permanence thus does not mean that things do not change, that time ceases. It means orderly change. Accordingly, there are two main sources for the disturbance of time: activities can either be finished too quickly and thus fail to reach their end or they can take too long and thus hinder the progress of time. Permanence is therefore based on the continuous supervision of correct endings and beginnings.

If beginnings and endings have such importance in the Daoist quest for permanence, then the question may arise: Does the Daoist "chain of time" have an "absolute" beginning in time—or maybe even outside of time—or does it resemble a circle without a beginning or end?

Some passages in the *Laozi* seem to indicate that time did indeed have a beginning. But this beginning, as we will see, does not really precede time. It is within temporality. Several passages in the *Laozi* discuss the issue of a "beginning," or of that which, as chapter 14 puts it, "in antiquity, was the beginning." Chapter 52 says:

> *The world has a beginning:*
> *it is considered the mother of the world.*

These lines resonate with the first chapter, which also talks about a "beginning" and a "mother." It seems as if time began sometime and then took on something like the shape of an arrow that reaches from a distant past to the present and into the future. But the fifty-second chapter of the *Laozi* does not proceed in such a linear fashion. It adds these quite cryptic words:

> *Return to the mother and preserve her,*
> *be unendangered by the transitoriness of the body.*

Obviously the *Laozi* asks for a return to that beginning which is considered to be "the mother of the world." And by this return, it is suggested, the "mother" will be "preserved" and one will be "unendangered by the transitoriness of the body." That it is possible to return to the beginning implies that time is understood as a circle, as a circle of becoming and passing. One might illustrate this notion with the Daoist image of the root. In autumn when it withers away, the plant "returns" to its mother—the root. And in this way the root is preserved. In the spring a new plant will continue the permanent circle of becoming and passing. The chain of time is a chain of continuous beginnings and endings. Every beginning becomes an ending, every ending becomes a beginning. The movement of time is a turning movement, and to return means to follow the course of permanent time. The "mother" of time—like the root of a plant—is constantly present at the center of this course, it is always "preserved." In this way the course of time is "unendangered by the transitoriness of the body" even though every single body is transitory. The transitoriness of every segment of time adds up to the constancy of time as a process. And thus chapter 52 concludes with the words:

> *This is called:*
> *following continuity.*

One "follows continuity" by "returning to the mother." This return takes place in all timely processes because every segment of time can be understood as a circle that returns to its beginning by ending. And every ending allows for a new beginning. Thus the Dao proceeds in a circle of continuous beginnings that never end. There is neither an absolute beginning nor an absolute ending. The Daoist beginning as described in the *Laozi*, cannot be determined, it is "hidden" because it continuously evades being fixed in the past. Chapter 14, which talks about the beginning in antiquity, also says:

> *Follow it—*
> *and you don't see its back.*
> *Approach it—*
> *and you don't see its head.*

The Daoist beginning is included in time. This beginning is not one that precedes or initiates time, but a beginning that is immersed in it. It is a beginning that is always included in the present.

The structure of permanence in the *Laozi* may be summarized as follows. First, there is the course of time as a continuous alternation of segments of time. Second, there is a "beginning" in the midst of the course of time that stabilizes and guarantees the orderliness and regularity of its course. This unceasing beginning is illustrated with such images as the root (in the midst of the growing and withering plant) or the hub (in the midst of the spokes circulating around it). In the realm of the segments of time there has to be timeliness—that is to say, the right beginning and the right end—so that all segments can seamlessly fit together. Each segment represents a stretch of presence. One stretch of presence connects to the next. The permanent course of time is a sequence of phases of presence. At the core of this sequence is a central "beginning" that continuously keeps the sequence going. This is the function of the hub within the wheel, but also of the ruler within the state when he issues the calendar and thus regulates the timeliness of all human activities. Perfect regularity is supposed to prevent any interruptions to the productive circulation of time. The fear of interruption is fought with an insistence on timeliness, and this timeliness is "supervised" by the non-present, non-beginning, and non-ending immanent center of time within the continuous course of its present, beginning, and ending phases.

The conception of time in the *Laozi* is considerably different from many of its conceptions in Western philosophy. It stands in particular contrast to St. Augustine's famous Christian conception of time as it is expressed in the eleventh book of the *Confessions*.[1] In the *Confessions*, Augustine reflects on the difference between secular temporality and divine eternity. The Word of God, the Creator, lets us experience this difference. The Word of God is eternal and silent, while our hearing of this Word is temporal. Augustine comments on how his own secular and temporal hearing of God's Word compares to God's Word itself: "It is far different, it is far different," he says, because the words that are heard "flee and pass away" while "the Word of my God abides above me forever."[2] In quite dramatic terms Augustine highlights the distinction between temporality and eternity, a distinction that is so deep that, in Augustine's words, when it comes to God "times are not coeternal with you, nor is any creature such, even if there were a creature above time" (303).

The distinction between divine eternity and secular temporality is paralleled by another distinction. Eternity goes along with "eternal Truth" (283). Eternal truth is not transitory. In relation to eternal truth, everything secular and temporal is potentially in "error." Since the distinction eternity/temporality is equated with the distinction truth/error, the way from "error" to truth is also the way from temporality to eternity—and, this is to say, to God as the "beginning." God is eternity and the beginning of temporality. To go toward God means to step toward eternity, toward the beginning, and toward truth and wisdom. Eternal wisdom, in Augustine's words, "shines through" the "dark clouds" of temporality and error (284).

At first sight, there seem to be some motifs in Augustine's philosophy of time that correspond to the *Laozi*. There is a distinction between a never-ending beginning and a passing temporality, and there is also an attempt to return to that beginning. These correspondences, however, are not substantial. While in the *Laozi* the enduring beginning is integrated into time, the divine beginning of Augustine is beyond the temporal. This difference between the *Laozi* and Augustine is the difference between permanence and eternity. While Augustine's eternity is time-transcending, Daoist permanence is time-immanent. As opposed to the *Laozi*, Augustine does not highly regard "long duration." In Augustine's view, long duration is but a bad copy of true eternity. To him, the temporal, however long it may last, is a mere shadow of "the splendor of that ever stable eternity." Compared to the ever stable eternity, even that which lasts long is merely a series of "many passing movements." The temporal can never be fully present because it is transitory and "passing." For Augustine only divine eternity is "wholly" and "ever present" (*semper est praesens*) (285), while in temporality even "a hundred years cannot be present" (289).

The difference between permanence in the *Laozi* and eternity in the *Confessions* is transformed into different attitudes toward time in Daoism and Christianity. Daoism affirms the full and lasting reality of the present, notwithstanding its transitoriness. In Christianity there is a tendency to not allow presence to be lasting and transitory at the same time. Full presence in Christianity has to be related to eternity and the transcendence of the merely temporal. In Daoism there is no devaluation of the passing of time and the passing of presence. Passing time is affirmed, and long (but not inappropriately long) duration is cherished. Daoism affirms the continuity of passing time, the permanence of change. Augustine, however, calls ongoing time a realm of "error" and of "dark clouds" which one has to "cut through." In the *Laozi*, true presence is located within temporality, in the *Confessions* it is the privilege of the trans-temporal God. The *Laozi* approves of duration and change, while the *Confessions* highlights the impurity of passing time.

Augustine points out that because past, present, and future always change into one another, then nothing is steady. If something would be truly steady, it would resemble the eternal and would no longer be temporal. Time, Augustine says,

> flies with such speed from future into the past that it cannot be extended by even a trifling amount. For if it is extended, it is divided into past and future. The present has no space. (289)

For us on earth and in time there is no "extended" presence. Such presence is only to be found in eternity. This is in stark contrast to the *Laozi*, where presence can well be extended in time. In the *Laozi* there is a continuous sequence of extended phases of presence, regulated by a non-presence at its center, with no eternal presence that is beyond temporality.

Even for Augustine there is, however, a sort of limited kind of presence within temporality. Temporal presence "happens" as the nonextended moment or instant. The presence of the instant can be experienced by the soul—the divine gift that humans received from God which connects them with him and eternity. In our soul or in our consciousness we measure time, and in it temporality becomes present to us. Only in our soul can we experience time as present, and only here can we overcome the distinction between the temporal and the eternal. The soul bridges the gap between humans and God.

Such Christian notions of the soul and of the "instant" are again alien to Daoist conceptions of time. In Augustine's Christian philosophy of time, the gap between eternity and temporality can be closed within the divine-human soul. The soul enables us to connect to the eternal in the temporal. But there is no such "mentalization" of time in Daoism because there is no need to bridge a gap between the temporal and the beyond. In Daoism, time is neither described as an experience of consciousness nor as something that has to do exclusively with human existence. "Cognitive," "phenomenological," or "existential" conceptions of time have been quite influential in the Western philosophical tradition, especially after Augustine—but they play virtually no role in Daoism. From a Christian perspective, time is related to eternity and therefore to the distinction between humans and God. Such a distinction is completely absent in Daoist "monism," and therefore time is neither something "mental" nor something "existential," and not even something "human." Time in the *Laozi* is nonhuman, it is a natural rhythm that allows everything to last and be present at the appropriate time.

CHAPTER 9

Death and the Death Penalty

Time and temporality are intrinsically connected with a major existential issue that practically all philosophies and religions deal with, namely the issue of the temporality of life or, more concretely, our "being toward death," our mortality. Death is thus, quite naturally, an important topic in the *Laozi*. Given its philosophy of permanence, the *Laozi* seems to identify the Dao with ongoing continuity and thus with the avoidance of death altogether. Chapter 6 claims that, "The spirit of the valley does not die." In a sense, the Dao seems to be "deathless," and to imitate the Dao may then mean for humans to practice deathlessness, to aspire to become immortal. It is precisely in this way that the *Laozi* has been understood by many Daoists, and the history of so-called religious Daoism (*dao jiao*) provides ample evidence for such interpretations. Daoist practice could mean the attempt to transform the body into an everlasting "organism," and Daoist practitioners developed innumerable remedies aimed at reaching this goal. In this way, the *Laozi* as a text could be read as a manual for overcoming death, and Laozi himself, its presumed author, could be revered as a model immortal who had successfully mastered that art.

The reading of the *Laozi* as a text on achieving immortality can certainly be justified with reference to such passages as the one from chapter

6 quoted above. However, such a reading is not necessarily in line with the philosophy of death as it was developed in other Daoist texts, most prominently the *Zhuangzi* as edited and commented on by Guo Xiang (d. 312 C.E.). Here, death is by no means something that can or should be avoided. On the contrary, death is given the same importance and acceptance as life. Here, the two phases are equally appreciated as segments of an "existential" sequence.[1] From this perspective, immortality is not a Daoist ideal and the *Laozi* is consequently not read in such a fashion. While the *Laozi* is still certainly interpreted as a text on permanence, this permanence is no longer associated with individual life or with the body, but with the continuous change of phases of life and death. In this way, longevity (*shou*), which has been so highly cherished not only in Daoism but in Chinese culture in general, is not so much understood as simply staying alive for as long as possible, but as a perpetual process of production and reproduction that integrates death rather than excluding it altogether—as chapter 33 of the *Laozi* says:

> *To die, but not to perish—*
> *this is longevity.*[2]

Read in the "spirit" of this verse, the many impressive passages in the *Laozi* that talk about life and death can be understood as illustrations of the permanent alternation of becoming and passing and not as somewhat "one-sided" praises of immortality. This is not to say that the *Laozi* does not recommend bodily cultivation and the care for one's life, but a philosophical reading should focus more on the equally present juxtaposition of life and death as complementary elements of a cycle of change. Chapter 76, for instance, depicts life and death in this way:

> *When alive,*
>   *men are supple and soft.*
> *When dead*
>   *they are, stretched out and reaching the end, hard and rigid.*
> *When alive*
>   *the ten thousand things and the grasses and trees,*

> *are supple and pliant.*
> *When dead,*
> *they are dried out and brittle.*
>
> *Therefore it is said:*
> *The hard and the rigid*
> *are the companions of death.*
> *The supple and the soft, the delicate and the fine*
> *are the companions of life.*

Obviously, life and death are different. Things transform when they change from life to death. What is dead is brittle, what is alive is elastic. But both stages are equally real and complementary. The brittle is not less actual than the elastic. The beginning of chapter 50 also talks about the "companions" of life and death, and it can be read in a similar way:

> *Going out into life.*
> *Going in into death.*
>
> *The companions of life are thirteen.*
> *The companions of death are thirteen.*
> *For the human beings moving on living their lives*
> *they all become thirteen spots of approaching death.*
> *And for which reason?*
> *Because they live their lives.*

In connection with chapter 76 these lines can be read as another illustration of the interdependence of life and death. Life and death substitute one another and thus belong together. A lifetime is followed by a "deathtime." Going out into life is at the same time going in into death. The Dao comprises both and, from its perspective, this circular movement is always going both out and in.

Seen in this light, to reach old age indicates, on the one hand, that one has lived one's life in a timely manner, i.e., that one did not end too soon but, on the other hand, it does not mean that one would become immortal. From this "philosophical" perspective, growing old only means not to die prematurely and thus not to interrupt natural temporality. This is different, for instance, from the "coercive and violent" man who lives dangerously and will thus likely "not meet his natural end," as chapter 42 states. In an ideal society, people will live long, but not endlessly. They will die at the right time. This is described in chapter 80 where it is said that people stay home and "reach old age and die."

While passages like the ones just mentioned do not suggest that death can be ultimately avoided, others seem to depict death as some sort of sickness or accident that may be prevented if one is only careful enough. Chapter 67, for instance, warns:

> *If one abandons staying back*
> *and goes to the front,*
> *one will die.*

Is this a strategy to live forever? Some chapters give even more detailed descriptions of states that seem to be "deathless." Chapter 50 says:

> *It is heard of those who are good at holding on to life:*
> *When they walk in the hills,*
> *they avoid neither rhinos nor tigers.*
> *When they go into battle,*
> *they carry no armor or weapons.*
> *The rhino has no spot to jab its horn.*
> *The tiger has no spot to put its claws.*
> *For the weapons there is no spot to lodge a blade.*
> *And for which reason?*
> *Because they have no spots of death.*

Are those interpreters of the *Laozi* correct who read the text as a manual for immortality? This does not necessarily have to be the case. All the images in the above passage illustrate how the Daoist sages will avoid friction, how they will not allow for the loss of energy, for any vulnerability in their bodies. This can be taken literally—as it was by many Daoist practitioners—but it can also be understood more figuratively. Then, it is not so much the individual being that becomes permanent, but the larger "body" of the community or of nature. If a state avoids friction, it will continue to exist—which does not mean that none of its inhabitants will die; if an army avoids friction, it will not be beaten—which does not mean that soldiers will not lose their lives; if people are careful in agriculture, nature will not be harmed—which does not mean that plants will not wither. "Life" may not be the life of individual people, but the larger cycle of life that is inclusive, not exclusive, of death. Social and natural "longevity" is then unharmed by the particular deaths that occur. In a "permanent" society and in the continuation of natural life, the death of individual beings does not threaten the well-being of the whole.

Read in this way, the *Laozi* does not aim at overcoming death, but rather at being able to affirm and endure it. Its conception of life accepts death as an equally real and natural phase. Biologically speaking, both life and death are equally valid segments in the process of vegetation. Every individual being that lives has to die. One cannot have life without death. But death is only harmful when viewed from the perspective of the individual being. If one is able to let go of that individualist perspective, then death loses its destructive meaning and becomes a moment of life. In this way, gaining immortality is equivalent to giving up one's individuality, with losing one's ego. By losing one's ego, one no longer sees life from such a narrow perspective. To put it in the words of chapter 67, which was quoted above: If one stays back, if one does not go to the front by developing an individual perspective and a specific ego, one can avoid the horror of death. If one is able to minimize one's consciousness of a self, there is nothing that is threatened by death. In other, more "metaphysical," words: If one identifies with the *process* of change rather than with individual substances, if one takes on an "ontology of process" rather than an "ontology of substances," then death loses its negativity.

Unlike in Christianity, death is not overcome by eternal life, it is rather accepted in its natural equality with life. In Christianity, the concept of the immortal soul allows for the survival of individual identity even after death. In Daoism, the strategy of coping with death is diametrically opposed. Here, it is not an indestructible individuality but, on the contrary, the total loss of individuality that eliminates the fear of death.

European philosophies of death in the Platonic or Christian tradition differ from the *Laozi* by overcoming death not "biologically" (by accepting it as an integral moment in the process of continuous reproduction), but "spiritually" (by conceiving of a non-bodily entity, such as the soul, which is indestructible). The concept of an immortal soul is present both in Plato and in Christianity, but not in the *Laozi*. There were concepts of a soul in ancient China and in Daoism, but these differed from the Platonic and Christian ones by neither assuming that the soul was absolutely single nor that it was imperishable. According to ancient Chinese beliefs, death dissolved not only bodily integration but also the "spiritual" integration of the soul. The soul could be dispersed just like the material body. Such conceptions, however, are not explicitly discussed in the *Laozi*. It is thus only important to note that, unlike in many influential "Western" religions and philosophies, death is not portrayed as a spiritual "liberation" from the body. For the *Laozi*, there is no overcoming of the biological by the spiritual in death. Quite the opposite is the case: In death, the biological wins out over the conscious perception of a self, and one will be less worried by death if one minimizes one's "spirituality" when alive.

The attitude toward death in the *Laozi* is affirmative because it is accepted as a natural phase within the cycle of biological reproduction. But there is also undoubtedly a fear of death—but this fear is not so much an "absolute" fear as it is "relative." What is feared is not so much death as such, but an untimely death, an unnatural death that occurs too early. If a plant that is supposed to wither in the fall withers in the summer, then this is perceived as worrisome. It indicates that something is wrong, that there have been mistakes in cultivation. The same is, of course, the case when it comes to human life. Sickness and an early death signal a wrong way of life. Death at an old age is natural and not to be feared; but when young, one should naturally be healthy. If one does not live out one's years, then this is a grave violation of the natural order because growing old is something that one is supposed to constantly take care of. Medical and hygienic practices were therefore always important not only in Daoism but in Chinese culture in general. There were, however, other dangers than illnesses. One could also be killed violently, for instance in war—but also by penal law. As in many cultures, the death penalty was a common practice, and while the *Laozi* does not talk about the immortality of the soul, it talks about the death penalty as an important "source" of untimely deaths.

That death was not so much feared in general, but more its untimely occurrence, was also reflected in the traditional Chinese penal system. Legal punishment, including capital punishment, was not only restricted to people of a certain minimum age, but there were also legal codes which applied a maximum age. This latter restriction was not so much established because of considerations of senility, but because of—besides the Confucian veneration of old age and the generally high social status of the elderly—the perhaps more Daoist conception that death at an old age was not a penalty but a natural thing.[3]

From a Daoist perspective, the severity of the death penalty is related to the absence of a belief in an eternal afterlife. The fear of an untimely death could in turn be used as a political instrument to establish "law and order" in the state. Capital punishment threatens offenders with death. Just as carelessness with respect to one's personal health could lead to an untimely death, the ruler could impose death on a person whose careless behavior threatened the health of society.

Capital punishment in Daoism was, just like medical practice, mainly preventative. If one did not prevent one's body from becoming sick, one was prone to die early. Likewise, a ruler's duty was to prevent "unhealthy" social phenomena, and one of the means for doing this was legal punishment. The ruler had to eliminate socially harmful behavior and could make use of the fear of an untimely death to establish a penal system based on deterrence. Prevention and deterrence are thus the two main components of the penal philosophy in the *Laozi*.

The preventive "logic" of the death penalty in the *Laozi* envisions a sort of chain-reaction of fear: The death penalty is established by the Daoist ruler (who manifests the Dao, the natural course of things) because of the fear of possible social harm. This then causes fear among the ruled, who want to avoid an early death. In this way the death penalty is supposed to eliminate itself: it will never have to be applied because the mechanism of fear will prevent wrongdoing. The death penalty in the *Laozi* thus works in the typical Daoist way: It acts through non-action. According to chapter 80 of the *Laozi*, in the ideal state people will be kept "afraid of death." On the other hand, chapter 75 explains that in a state where "people are difficult to govern," they will "treat death lightly." A state where death and the death penalty are not feared is bound to decay. It will perish like a body that does not fear illness.

In the first part of chapter 74 the Daoist use of the death penalty is explained in more detail:[4]

> *If the people are not at all afraid of death,*
>   *how should they be frightened by the death penalty?*
> *If people are at all afraid of death,*
>   *and if I will capture and execute those who act wrongly,*
>   *who then will dare to do so?*
> *If the people are to fear death at all,*
>   *then there always has to be a hangman.*

The hangman is indispensable to the rule of the Daoist ruler, but because he is there, there will be no need for him to take action. The Daoist ruler, the "I" in the text, is the only one who has the power to execute, because he is supposed to manifest the Dao and to have an "empty heart." That is to say, he does not have any personal inclinations or emotions. The death penalty is not a mechanism for an individual exercise of power. It is a "natural" instrument for creating social order and not a tool for rulers with personal interests. The Daoist death penalty functions, so to speak, in a "self-so" (*ziran*) way: It functions without any "subjective" intentions, and its functioning is totally non-active: It creates order without actually being used.

Of course, there was always the danger that the death penalty might be abused by a non-Daoist ruler who gave reign to personal emotions and used the death penalty actively in order to exercise personal power. If this happened, the paradoxical effect of the Daoist death penalty would be reversed. If someone with a personal "will to power" made use of the death penalty, then it would become, because of its application, a useless tool. It would lead to violence, disorder, and revolt. In the end, the tyrant would likely become a victim of the penalty he tried to use in his own interests—he would be punished by the people who rose up against him. This is illustrated in the second part of chapter 74:

> *Well,*
> *intending to replace the hangman in hanging,*
> *this is to replace the wood cutter in cutting wood.*
> *When the wood cutter is replaced,*
> *the hand is seldom unharmed.*

The Daoist hangman is a hangman who does not hang. If he is replaced by a hangman who hangs, and who hangs with a purpose, this will result in the hangman himself finally being hanged.

The Daoist death penalty is solely based on deterrence. There is personal edge to it, neither on the side of the executioner nor on that of the offender. It is totally preventative, it does not aim at "retribution." It wants to discourage crime rather than to revenge it. Moreover, it is neither moral nor emotional. It is not based on a "morality of anger" but, rather, tries to exclude all emotionality. It is concerned with the effectiveness of social processes, not with individual "justice." The use of the death penalty was mainly concerned with the practical effects of the penalty, with its social results. It aimed mainly at preventing bad deeds, not at punishing the evil or revenging the innocent.

Deterrence was, of course, also a reason for defending capital punishment in the "West"—but it was hardly seen as *essential* as it appears in the *Laozi*. In the Western tradition, the death penalty used to be (and still is in many states of the United States) justified rather non-daoistically with respect to the persons involved. Friedrich Nietzsche, the great "deconstructionist" of the Christian tradition, has described this tendency quite eloquently. To him, Christianity developed a "metaphysics of the hangman," which conceived of the human being as free and guilty at the same time. By constructing man as having a free will and thus as being a free agent, individual persons could at the same time be described as individually responsible and therefore as potentially guilty *sinners*. According to Nietzsche, Western theologians invented "free will" to "contaminate the innocence of becoming with 'punishment' and 'guilt.' "[5] The freer humans are, the guiltier they become. There is an immediate correlation between the semantics of freedom and the semantics of guilt.

When a Western metaphysics of capital punishment characterizes the offender as an individual sinner who is *evil* and not only a *wrong*doer who did something *bad*, then it is no longer the action that is of concern and that the punishment is related to, but rather the offender as a human being. This is a total reversal of the Daoist model that is found in the *Laozi*. Now the main concern is no longer to prevent certain actions, but rather to exact revenge and destroy evil people. The focus on the victim that is so prominent in contemporary death penalty practice is an immediate reflection of this status of revenge. The punishment is supposed to "bring closure" to the victims or their relatives. While the metaphysics of the hangman in the *Laozi* is one of prevention, the Christian version is one of *ressentiment* toward the offender—to use another Nietzschean term.[6]

Even though the Daoist death penalty aims at having no executions, it is obviously neither "milder" nor more "merciful" than its Western counterpart. These categories belong to the specific Christian tradition criticized by Nietzsche, and they are supplements of the semantics of justice and retribution and represent an integral part of it. The Daoist death penalty is nonmoralistic and nonemotional. It is therefore not "better" than a Christian philosophy of the death penalty. What then is it good for?

One thing that it may be good for is that it helps one see the contingency of the semantics of guilt and free will and their relation to a semantics of punishment and justice that is presently applied to legal killings. I do not think that one should trust these semantics, even though they are used to justify not only certain penal systems but even foreign policies and military action. If one looks at it philosophically, it turns out to be historically and culturally contingent. Although I consider it an outdated philosophical rhetoric, I do not advocate replacing it with a probably even more outdated Daoist one. Still, I think that a reflection on Daoism helps to understand the dubiousness of some still-surviving traditional philosophical notions. A comparative reflection of this kind may promote a sense of philosophical decency and modesty when it comes to decisions about taking life. It is probably at times advisable for philosophy to refrain from providing the hangmen with a metaphysics. Why not just leave them without one?

CHAPTER 10

"Without the Impulses of Man"
A DAOIST CRITIQUE OF HUMANISM

Toward the end of chapter 5 in the *Zhuangzi* there is the following dialogue between Zhuangzi and his friend Hui Shi:

> Said Hui Shi to Zhuangzi: "Can a man really be without the impulses of man?"
> "He can."
> "If a man is without the impulses of man, how can we call him a man?"
> "The Dao gives him the guise, heaven gives him the shape, how can we refuse to call him a man?"
> "But since we do call him a man, how can he be without the impulses of man?"
> "Judging 'That's it, that's not' is what I mean by 'the impulses of man.' What I mean by being without the impulses is that the man does not inwardly wound his person by likes and dislikes, that he constantly goes by the spontaneous and does not add anything to the process of life."[1]

The Daoist sages are at the fringes of humanity. Outwardly they look like humans and live in their company, but they are more companions of "heaven" than companions of men. By nature, man is human—therefore the sages have a human shape. But by nature humans are also natural, and the sages are able to develop this larger nature within themselves to such a degree that their "humanity" does not affect their being simply natural.

What I translated as "the impulses" of man in the above passage is *qing* in the original, a term that is otherwise often translated as "feeling" or "emotion."[2] The "emotional" quality of human beings is certainly associated here with *qing*—and I chose the term "impulses" to include such connotations. The specific explanation of *qing* given by the *Zhuangzi*, however, is slightly different from a purely "psychological" meaning. The *Zhuangzi* says twice that what is meant by *qing* is the human *judgmental attitude*, the tendency to either approve of disapprove, to say "it is so" or "it is not so" (*shi* and *fei* in Chinese). This particular attitude is apparently, at least in this short dialogue, what constitutes the particular "human" aspect that is overcome by the sage—and by the sage alone (in "solitude").

The attitudes of approving or disapproving, of liking and disliking, are those that make humans special—both generically and individually. Generically, the human species is probably the only one that cognitively distinguishes between what is right and what is wrong, between what is true and what is false. These distinctions indeed distinguish man from the rest of nature. But, maybe even more importantly, it is also by these attitudes that individuals distinguish themselves from other individuals. We are different from each other by having different likes and dislikes, by having different opinions and adhering to different truths. It is through our ability to judge that we develop individuality and that we can differentiate ourselves from others. This is maybe, at least from the perspective of the *Zhuangzi*, the most important philosophical aspect of having likes and dislikes: by them we distinguish ourselves as humans.

The Daoist sages acknowledge these human characteristics and do not aim at abolishing them. However, they remain untouched by them. Alone, in "solitude," is the sage able to refrain from distinguishing him- or herself by these distinctive judgments. Only in this way can the sage remain truly and universally affirmative. Only by not siding with any specific affirmation that would necessarily include a specific negation can the sage affirm *everything*. The Daoist sage is thus not an "*over*man," but rather an "*under*man" who remains below the threshold of human individuation—as opposed to all other human individuals. The sage "takes on the place which the mass of the people detest" (to use the words of chapter 8 of the *Laozi*) and dispenses with any ambition to be distinct. It is, in typically paradoxical Daoist fashion, by this total renunciation of any human distinction that the sages distinguish themselves from all humans.

The Daoist sage is, in other words, the only human who is free from human vanity, free from the impulse to determine what is right and what is wrong—and this can be understood in any sense: aesthetically, morally, emotionally, "scientifically." The sage is the only human who has no desire to prefer, for instance, the beautiful over the ugly, to label this as good and that as evil, to find dying emotionally more disturbing than living, to deem one opinion as correct and another as incorrect. This does not mean that Daoist sages would deny these human distinctions, but they do not "inwardly wound their persons" with them. The sage is thus not humane—and therefore all the more natural—and the above passage from the *Zhuangzi* can well be understood as an illustration of the following lines from chapter 5 of the *Laozi*:

> *Heaven and earth are not humane.*
> *They regard the ten thousand things as straw dogs.*
> *The sage is not humane.*
> *He regards all the people as straw dogs.*[3]

Instead of being "humane," the Daoist sage rather takes on the attitude of heaven and earth and treats human beings like "straw dogs" (*chu gou*). Straw dogs, as ancient and modern commentators point out in unison,[4] were highly revered elements in sacrificial rituals, but after the ritual they lost all their meaning and were simply discarded. A passage in the *Zhuangzi* explains: "Before the straw dogs are laid out for the sacrifice, they are packed in bamboo boxes wrapped in patterned brocades, and the medium and the priest fast and do austerities before escorting them. But once the sacrifice is over, nothing remains for them but to have their heads and spines trampled by the passers-by, or be gathered as fuel for the kitchen stove."[5] Thus, the Daoist sage does not seem to care much for people—at least not once they are dead.

Given this context, I believe that this fifth chapter of the *Laozi* can be read as an attack against Confucian and "humanist" ritualism. Rituals, especially those having to do with death, were of the utmost importance for Confucian culture. The mentioning of cast-away straw dogs ridicules the ritual performance. Obviously, the ritual, which is supposed to celebrate permanence—the permanence of human ancestors and the clan—is a highly impermanent event. Once the ritual is over, the ritual objects lose all their meaning.

Here, the *Laozi* seems to criticize the Confucian quest for human permanence as a failure. From a Daoist perspective, permanence cannot be based on a celebration of an ongoing presence (of the ancestors and the clan) but only on the recognition of incessant change. Human beings are not permanent, and the Confucian ritual does not make them so. Second, from a Daoist perspective the Confucian ritual seems to express an unacceptable emotional seizure by life and death. Like the *Zhuangzi*, the *Laozi* criticizes the Confucian emotional obsession with death. For a Daoist, such an emotional attachment, arising from human tendencies to prefer life over death, is as "unnatural" as the emotional attachment to a straw dog—whom even the Confucians happily discard once the ritual is over.

While I think that the image of the straw dog criticizes and mocks Confucian ritualism, I believe what, above all, is at issue here is the "humanism" tied to it. Like heaven and earth, the Daoist sage is not especially "humane" and not particularly concerned with human beings. For the Daoist sage, human beings are not essentially different from dogs—not even from *straw dogs*! Human beings vanish from life just as straw dogs from a ritual performance. Just as straw dogs turn into fuel for the fireplace, human beings will not turn into heavenly ancestors but, rather (for instance), something as nonhuman as the wood for a crossbow, to use an image from the *Zhuangzi*.[6] The Daoist sage—who in the second part of chapter 5 of the *Laozi* is compared to a nonhuman bellows—is not only indifferent toward human death but also indifferent to human beings altogether. This is, of course, not to say that sages dislike or even despise humankind; they are simply not more or less attached to this species than to any other. In emptying themselves, sages not only empty themselves of emotions, they also empty themselves of gender and species.

The non-humanist philosophy of the *Laozi* goes along with a non-humanist literary form. As discussed in my introductory chapter, the *Laozi* was not really written or composed for "people" to read. It was aimed at a very limited audience—there were initially only very few persons to whom it was addressed, i.e., the prospective (sage-) rulers. Its style was hermetic and certainly as inaccessible to most of ancient China as it is today in the West. Its "educational" function was very different from a humanist ideal which looks upon wisdom as something that should be spread as widely as possible. The Western "enlightenment" was supposed to at least gradually extend knowledge to everyone. There is no such educational purpose discernible in the *Laozi*, the text obviously does not make any attempt at being generally intelligible.

The *Laozi* is not only not addressed to humans in general, it also does not speak with a discernible human voice. Earlier interpretations of the text and, particularly, early Western translations have read the *Laozi* as if there was an individual author expressing his thoughts. This led to more hermeneutical problems than solutions. There is scarcely an "I" that speaks in the text, and when there is, it does not appear to be the "I" of a narrator but, rather, the "I" of a reader or listener who is supposed to identify with what is said. Given the absence of such a personal voice, there is also no specific "intention" that would hold the text together; there is no linear story, no development of argumentation. To make such assumptions would mean to "humanize" a text that does not have a "humanist" form— and this would be a hermeneutical error. Individual authorship and the notion of a general readership are modern Western ideas and thus, in a certain sense, humanist categories that do not apply to the *Laozi*.

The lack of such basic "humanist" elements in the literary structure of the *Laozi* leads to the further non-humanist characteristics of the text. It does not have a fixed form or shape. There is no "original" that would represent a definite version of the text. The text evolved, so to speak, "self-so." This does not mean that there were no actual people who wrote the text down, but these people, as individuals, cannot be identified as authors. The inability to identify an author, in the strict sense of this term, results in the inability to identify a particular authoritative form of the text. The *Laozi* "morphed" itself continuously, and the most advanced translations reflect exactly this. The translation by Roger T. Ames and David Hall,[7] for instance, comes along with a Chinese text that never existed—it is a collation of different versions, including the newly discovered ancient manuscripts as well as the "classical" commentaries. From a traditional "humanist" philological perspective, Ames and Hall can thus be accused of a sacrilege—they violated the principle of identifying an "original"—but in the case of the *Laozi*, I would argue in their defense. All attempts to identify an original reflect a "humanist" prejudice.

Chapters 3, 4, and 5 of the present volume have explored how the *Laozi* presents a non-humanist picture of a realm that appears to "modern man" intrinsically human. Society, in the *Laozi*, is not primarily human but embedded and included in cosmic processes. The agrarian society of ancient China did not so much depend on human deeds as it depended on such phenomena as the weather. There was not much that men could do when there was a drought or an earthquake. Human life had to follow the rhythm of "heaven and earth"—the rhythm of Yin and Yang—rather than impose itself on nature. In the larger cosmic functioning, the realm of men was only existent within the realms of heaven and earth, and from this perspective an isolated humanist concept even of human society would be one-sided or "abstract." Heaven and earth cannot be bracketed when it comes to human life, and society has to be understood in terms of nature rather than the other way around.

The interdependence between cosmic and human processes is particularly conspicuous in the *Laozi* with respect to an issue that is often presented as exclusively human in our times. Sexuality, from the perspective of the *Laozi*, is cosmic rather than human, and procreation is a larger issue within which human fertility is only a moment. Without the continuous renewal of the seasons and the renewed life of plants and animals, human procreation would be impossible.

Given these circumstances, the ruling of men, or human politics, cannot be undertaken without the consideration of cosmic processes. Human "culture" cannot be isolated from "nature"—there is no "humanist" dichotomy between nature and culture to begin with. Order within the state is a moment within the larger cosmic order, and the principles of order that apply in one realm are the same that apply in another. The sage-ruler in the *Laozi* is less preoccupied with human issues—unlike the ruler in models envisioned in early Western modernity, like that of the Leviathan who has to rule out of specifically human concerns and because of specifically human interests—than with mediating between man and nature, operating as a link between society and the cosmos. The sage-ruler is not so much a man among men as the pivot of the volatile and delicate balance between heaven, man, and earth.

In this book, chapters 6, 7, 8, and 9 deal with psychological and cognitive aspects of human existence. In these areas, the *Laozi* advocates methods of minimizing or decreasing activity that come close to a dehumanization of the humane. The Daoist sage is depicted as a human being that lacks specifically human characteristics, such as desires, intentions, emotions, and judgments. As a link between the human realm and heaven and earth, the sage becomes as indifferent to human categories as these two realms naturally are. Heaven and earth do not "care"—and neither does the Daoist sage in the *Laozi*. But this absence of care is not "carelessness," it is quite the opposite. It is the condition for a smooth and thus frictionless integration of the human world into the larger cosmos. The emotional and cognitive inactivity of the sages is the very condition not only for an impartial rule of the state but, more importantly, for their ability to not interfere in what goes on "self-so" (*ziran*). Only by emptying themselves of their selves can the sage-rulers be without any personal or individual concerns that would necessarily result in a "conflict of interests" and thus infringe upon the harmony in the world.

The nonhuman (non-)qualities of the sage integrate humans seamlessly into the world. This results in a world of pure immanence. The sage practically manifests the immanence of humankind. There is nothing human left which is "transcendent" with respect to the world. Man is not created in the image of a transcendent God with an inbuilt capacity to cognitively—through "ideas"—transcend the "material." There is no program to subdue nature, nor is there any kind of superiority attached to humans. The human realm functions as "organically" or, if one prefers this metaphor, "machinically" as the rest of the cosmos.

By holding their human "impulses" in check, the sages hold the human impulses of all humankind in check. The sages do not function as saviors of mankind, taking all human "sins" upon themselves, but (at least in the political philosophy of the *Laozi*) give up their human characteristics for the benefit of all others. This is remarkably different from the Christian model. Through Jesus Christ, God became human, and He took on distinctively human features in order to save and ennoble all humans. This Christian model of humanization seems to be the exact opposite of the Daoist strategy. The *Laozi* aims at serving humankind through an ideal being who reduces all human "impulses."

The non-humanist philosophy of the *Laozi* may seem quite unattractive to readers accustomed to modern Western humanism. Christianity is, in practically all its variations, a thoroughly humanist religion, and while the Enlightenment tended to dispense with the religious "superstructure," religious values were often secularized so that the humanist core was not only preserved but even amplified or condensed. Concepts such as "human rights," or "human dignity," are clearly humanistic, but also notions such as "freedom" and "liberty," "democracy" and "justice," and even more concrete ideals such as "education" and "health," are deeply humanist and enjoy great public prestige in current Western societies. These terms, along with many related ones, constitute the dominant semantics in contemporary society, and there is not much in the *Laozi* that would connect to them. On the contrary, the non-humanist philosophy of the *Laozi* is often diametrically opposed to these semantics. Is the *Laozi* therefore a philosophical "scandal" in our times? Should it be discarded like a straw dog because the ritual in which it served is no longer practiced? I don't think so. While the *Laozi* can certainly not be taken "literally" and while its non-humanist teachings cannot be immediately adopted in our times, it can still function as an important contribution to the attempts at overcoming some outdated humanist self-descriptions that are still prevalent.

While humanist semantics still dominates public discourse and opinion in Western societies, it has, even here, lost a lot of its philosophical credibility. A philosophical revolt against the humanist vocabulary dates back to at least Friedrich Nietzsche, whose famous or notorious "overman" is not so much a superhuman or "superman," but a novel concept of the human that goes beyond narrow humanist categories. Nietzsche's non-humanism has been taken up by some of the most influential contemporary thinkers, particularly in so-called Continental philosophy. Michel Foucault's book *The Order of Things* begins with a fictional, but nonetheless quite realistic, description of a Chinese encyclopedia which represents a decisively non-Western and non-humanist way of categorizing reality, and it ends with the conclusion that "man is neither the oldest nor the most constant problem that has been posed for human knowledge." The modern concept of man is a European invention of the sixteenth century. If our society changes again, Foucault states, "then one can certainly wager that man would be erased, like a face drawn in sand at the edge of the sea."[8]

Man has become, at least since the Enlightenment, a "fundamental arrangement" of our knowledge, of our way of making sense of the world. However, as Foucault has shown, this arrangement is not "natural," but historically contingent. It is not necessary to describe the world in human terms, and there is no guarantee at all that human terms are the most adequate for such a description. Other postmodern authors, such as Gilles Deleuze, have further expanded Foucault's criticism and presented new and often irritating philosophical concepts—such as the "rhizome"— which are clearly non-humanist but, rather, "organic" or "machinic." It seems that while the philosophy of the *Laozi* is strongly at odds with modern Western humanism, it is sometimes quite akin to current developments in post-humanist thought. This is, if one takes Foucault's words seriously, not astonishing. If the "thick" humanism of the modern Western world is a historical phenomenon, then it cannot be a surprise that other traditions do not share it—and thus are, at least with respect to what they are not, comparable to postmodern developments. I would claim that the coincidences between Daoism and postmodern philosophies are the coincidences between a pre-humanist and a post-humanist philosophy. That there are such parallels is not so surprising—if simply because neither of them is humanist. And because the humanist semantics is still so pervasive, these parallels may stick out quite conspicuously. In other words, the pre-humanist *Laozi* and post-humanist authors like Foucault and Deleuze may be perceived as equally "scandalous." And they may both contribute to erasing that face in the sand—which will not be to the delight of those who are still playing on that beach.

One may trace back the "contemporary" relevance of the non-humanist *Laozi* along the lines of the above division of issues: textual, social, and cognitive-psychological.

In the first chapter of this book I compared the textual characteristics of the *Laozi* to present-day hypertext. Rather than the traditional "humanist" linear development of a text by which a single author addresses an audience, the *Laozi* represents an open textual structure. Such open structures become increasingly the norm in our society. While (hopefully, with respect to the present instance) books are still read, other textual forms are on the rise. On the Internet, traditional human forms of communication are no longer practiced. Conversations are made by using multiple pseudonyms, and the codes of communication become so extremely specialized that a high degree of familiarity with a "technical" language is necessary for participation. No individual human authorship can be identified in these discourses. A plurality of heterogeneous discourses emerges, and the discourses seem to function systemically by generating their own rules.

Even traditional media have become more and more standardized. Soap operas are written collectively, and the individual writer is replaceable—and continuously replaced. So-called "reality TV" is by no means "real" in the traditional sense but, to use Baudrillard's term, a simulated reality that does not reflect a human reality outside the media. Even when one watches a news channel, one is not confronted with an "individual" communicative product, but with a variety of information "performed" on several parallel layers: spoken commentary, different written texts simultaneously displayed, visual information, and so on. The "human" element in the types of communication which take up such a large part of contemporary society is hardly discernible.

The areas that arguably produce the largest volume of text in contemporary society are the mass media and the Internet. Their textual production can hardly be properly analyzed with traditional humanist concepts. Most of today's texts are no longer written like Dickens's novels or Kant's philosophical works once were. Traditionally, such textual products were studied within the "humanities," but this very concept becomes increasingly obsolete with respect to the understanding of texts. The humanities were called humanities in the spirit of the Enlightenment, which conceived of texts as products of and for subjectivity. But these premises are no longer generally valid. The mass media of the twenty-first century are hardly instances of "subjectivity," and new academic disciplines or methodologies have to be invented to study these phenomena.

Given these drastic changes, it may be assumed that the traditional categories of literary analysis will not necessarily dominate the reception of such texts as the *Laozi* forever. It may well turn out that, on the basis of a post-humanist hermeneutics, the pre-humanist *Laozi* will appear in a new light. And, perhaps, the new study of ancient pre-humanist texts may even help to develop a future post-humanist hermeneutics.

Probably even more shocking to contemporary readers than its textual characteristics are the social and political aspects of the *Laozi*. The *Laozi* does not look at society as a community of individuals, and it does not suggest that humans look for creative ways to organize their community politically so that it will be just and beneficial. In short, the *Laozi* does not view society as being constituted by human agency. Even, and particularly, the most powerful human being in society, the sage-ruler, does *not act*.

While the lack of human agency certainly goes against the dominating description of current society, I am not so sure if it is actually so much at odds with social reality. Although humans in a "free" society certainly tend to conceive of themselves as having some control over society, one may, as in the Daoist state, doubt if the politically powerful actually shape society through their agency. Even presidents and governments cannot steer events. While they can make decisions, it is always unclear what these decisions will actually bring about. A government may introduce a new law, but there is no guarantee that this will result in what was intended. Another government may go to war, but it may well be that this decision fails to bring about the desired results. Human agency is taken for granted, but it is by no means clear that what happens in society is actually a direct effect of the actions of political decision makers. Maybe it is not entirely outlandish to presume, as the *Laozi* does, that the function of political power and leadership is, in a certain sense, more symbolic than practical. Leaders manifest the unity of a society and give the impression that an order is established and that rules are in place. But it is not clear, despite the dominating semantics, if political leaders are actually able to literally *lead* society.

There may be a similar lack of human agency in the functioning of the economy. The mechanisms of the so-called market are often not really traceable to the specific economic decisions of individuals. There is no specific person or group that the rise or fall of a currency, of inflation or deflation, can be attributed to. Even if, looking back, one is used to ascribing such developments to certain people or decisions—let's say to the tax-cut of a government—these claims are highly dubious. If it were really in the power of politicians or other human beings to steer the economy as economic agents, why would recessions occur? The tendency to ascribe economic developments to human decisions after the fact may rather prove the human will to such ascriptions than actual human economic agency.

The potential for human agency in the psychological and cognitive realm may also be questioned—both from an ancient Daoist pre-humanism as well as from a current post-humanist perspective. It was once more Friedrich Nietzsche (and later, in his footsteps, Sigmund Freud) who identified the amount of human vanity that is attached to such notions as a "free will." The free will that the modern Western "enlightenment" valued so highly may be merely a minor component of our actual psychological setup. The "ego" is more a construct or product of consciousness than its actual "master." There are uncontrollable drives and instincts, and there is an inaccessible unconscious in relation to which our "ego" seems to be rather powerless. As modern experimental psychology has shown, there are many actions that, though we ascribe them to our willful agency, we in fact perform automatically—and only by doing so can we perform them well.[9] We learn to drive a car by learning not to continuously think about how to drive. We learn to reduce conscious decisions to a minimum so that the traffic can flow. The orderly flow of traffic depends on the minimization of individual "egos" involved in driving. The *Laozi* envisions a similar automatic flow in society by decreasing the ego-focus of humans.

I am not convinced that a pre- or post-humanist philosophical outlook is more attractive than a humanist one. Freud's "relativization" of the ego has rightly been called the third insult to human vanity (after Copernicus who showed that we are not at the center of the cosmos and Darwin who showed that we were not present at the beginning of creation), and to have one's vanity insulted often makes one feel uncomfortable. The humanist vision of the world is perhaps more likable, more sympathetic, and more flattering than the pre- and post-human alternatives. But one may still opt for the latter for a very human reason: the non-humanist view seems to be a more sincere and modest self-description, a self-description which not only takes into account what humans can or should be able to do, but also what they can't and therefore maybe shouldn't pretend to do. That at least, and at last, saves humans a lot of trouble.

APPENDIX I

A Note on the Textual History of the *Daodejing*

The textual history of the *Laozi* or *Daodejing* is very complex and its early stages are largely unknown. The oldest extant manuscripts of the text were discovered as recently as 1993 in an ancient tomb in the Chinese town of Guodian. These manuscripts contain parts of the later standard edition or *textus receptus* and were written around 300 B.C.E. It is generally assumed that the text, or at least its contents, stem from older oral traditions of, perhaps, various origins.

The second oldest manuscripts were discovered two decades earlier and date back to around 200 B.C.E. They were found in a tomb in a place called Mawangdui and contain two nearly complete versions of the later *textus receptus*.

Neither of the ancient manuscripts indicates an author or a general title for the text. It is known that there were editions and commentaries in the time of the Han dynasty (206 B.C.E.–220 C.E.), but today we have no complete version of the text from this period. It was originally known under the name of Laozi, its presumed author. During the Han dynasty, it was given the honorific title "The Classical Scripture of the Way and Its Efficacy" or *Daodejing*.

The *textus receptus* of the *Laozi* is the edition by Wang Bi (226–249 C.E.). Wang Bi's *Laozi*, along with his philosophical commentary, significantly influenced the history of the text, many of its later interpretations, and, in more recent times, translations into other languages. Contemporary research, however, suggests that the Wang Bi edition as it is known today is not the original one.

A concise history of the text by Roger T. Ames and David Hall is contained in their *Daodejing: "Making This Life Significant": A Philosophical Translation* (New York: Ballantine, 2003), 1–10. Another recommended academic overview of the textual history (excluding the Guodian manuscripts) is William G. Boltz, "Lao tzu Tao te ching," in Michael Loewe, ed., *Early Chinese Texts: A Bibliographical Guide* (Berkeley: The Society for the Study of Early China and The Institute of East Asian Studies, University of California, Berkeley, 1993), 269–92.

APPENDIX 2

A Note on English Translations of the *Daodejing*

The translations listed below are all, for various reasons, recommended. They are either of historical interest in documenting the Western—and particularly the philosophical—reception of their time, or represent the most recent scholarship, and/or are, in my view, of a high literary or academic standard. The list is chronological.

There are certainly other fine translations which are not included in this list, but there are also many translations of dubious quality (from an academic point of view) on the market. When reading the text, it is beneficial to compare several translations—they often vary greatly.

I have published a German translation of the Mawangdui manuscripts of the *Laozi* (*Laotse: Tao Te King: Nach den Seidentexten von Mawangdui* [Frankfurt am Main: Fischer, 1995]). An English version will be published by Open Court (Chicago).

ROGER T. AMES AND DAVID HALL. *Daodejing: "Making This Life Significant": A Philosophical Translation*. New York: Ballantine, 2003.

As the title says, this translation presents the text from a philosophical perspective. It contains a highly recommended introduction, definitions of core philosophical terms, and a scholarly analysis of the Guodian texts.

RUDOLPH G. WAGNER. *A Chinese Reading of the Daode jing: Wang Bi's Commentary on the Laozi with Critical Text and Translation.* Albany: State University of New York Press, 2003.

This is more a sinological study than a translation. It is only recommended for scholars.

PHILIP J. IVANHOE. *The Daodejing of Laozi.* Indianapolis and Cambridge: Hackett, 2002.

This very readable translation takes recent scholarship into account and includes an appendix that compares various translations of the first chapter.

ROBERT G. HENRICKS. *Lao Tzu's Tao Te Ching: A Translation of the Startling New Documents Found at Guodian.* New York: Columbia University Press, 2000.

This edition contains a detailed analysis and scholarly translation of the materials unearthed at Guodian. The appendix includes a translation of Sima Qian's "Biography" of Laozi, a line-by-line comparison of the Guodian texts with the Mawangdui and Wang Bi variants, and a description of the punctuation marks and chapter divisions.

RICHARD JOHN LYNN. *The Classic of the Way and Virtue: A New Translation of the Tao-Te Ching of Laozi as Interpreted by Wang Bi.* New York: Columbia University Press, 1999.

This translation of Wang Bi's commentary on the *Laozi* includes a detailed and interesting study on Wang Bi as well as a translation of Wang Bi's "Outline Introduction to the *Laozi*" (*Laozi zhilüe*).

VICTOR H. MAIR. *Tao Te Ching: The Classic Book of Integrity and the Way.* New York: Quality Paperback Book Club, 1998.

This very readable translation by a sinologist is based on the Mawangdui manuscripts. In the afterword, the translator analyzes the oral background of the text and tries to prove connections between the *Laozi* and ancient Indian Hindu practices and texts. This hypothesis is, to my knowledge, not generally accepted.

MICHAEL LAFARGUE. *Tao and Method: A Reasoned Approach to the Tao Te Ching*. Albany: State University of New York Press, 1994.

This book is a detailed study of the *Laozi* and its historical background. The author develops his own hermeneutical approach.

ROBERT G. HENRICKS. *Lao-Tzu: Te-Tao Ching: A New Translation Based on the Recently Discovered Ma-Wang-Tui Texts*. New York: Ballantine, 1989.

This edition presents the transcribed Mawangdui manuscripts along with a chapter-by-chapter commentary that focuses on philological analyses.

D. C. LAU. *Lao Tzu: Tao Te Ching*. London: Penguin, 1963; and Hong Kong: Chinese University of Hong Kong Press, 1982.

The Penguin edition is widely available, very readable, and contains Lau's influential analysis of the oral origins of the text. The Hong Kong edition contains a translation of the Mawangdui manuscripts.

R. Y. W. YOUNG AND ROGER T. AMES (translators); CHEN GUYING (author). *Lao Tzu: Text, Notes, and Comments*. San Francisco: Chinese Materials Center, 1981.

This edition introduces an annotated and commented edition of the *Laozi*. It provides an insight into modern Chinese scholarship on the text.

ARIANE RUMP AND WING-TSIT CHAN. *Commentary on the Lao Tzu by Wang Pi*. Honolulu: University of Hawaii Press, 1979.

This edition contains Wing-tsit Chan's translation of the *Laozi* along with a translation of the Wang Bi commentary that highlights its philosophical relevance.

PAUL J. LIN. *A Translation of Lao-tzu's Tao Te Ching and Wang Pi's Commentary*. Ann Arbor: University of Michigan Center for Chinese Studies, 1977.

This translation introduces Wang Bi's commentary.

WING-TSIT CHAN. *The Way of Lao Tzu*. Indianapolis: Bobbs-Merrill, 1963.

Chan's translation presents the text in a quite "metaphysical" light. This translation greatly influenced the philosophical reception of the text.

EDUARD ERKES. *Ho-shang-kung's Commentary on Lao-tse*. Ascona: Artibus Asiae, 1950.

The Heshanggong commentary is, next to Wang Bi's commentary, the most important traditional Chinese version of the text and particularly influenced the practice of Daoism in China.

ARTHUR WALEY. *The Way and Its Power: A Study of the Tao Te Ching*. London: Allen and Unwin, 1934.

This "classical" translation was also highly influential for the reception of the text. It presents the text in a poetic fashion.

JAMES LEGGE. *The Texts of Taoism: The Tao Teh King; The Tao and Its Characteristics*. Oxford: Oxford University Press, 1891.

This translation reflects the earlier reception of the text by Western missionary scholars.

Notes

Preface: The Philosophy *of the* Daodejing

1. Warren Frisina and Gary DeAngelis, eds., *Teaching the Daodejing* (Oxford: Oxford University Press, forthcoming.)
2. Mencius 3A.4, quoted from the translation by D. C. Lau, *Mencius* (London: Penguin, 1970), 101 (translation modified).
3. See appendix 1.
4. After completing the manuscript of this book I became aware of a brilliant book that presents a novel non-humanist and "Neo-Daoist" philosophy in our times: John Gray's *Straw Dogs: Thoughts on Humans and Other Animals* (London: Granta, 2002). I highly recommend it to anybody who is interested in the contemporary relevance of Daoist ideas.

1 How to Read the Daodejing

1. See appendix 1 for a textual history of the *Laozi*.
2. See appendix 1.
3. I will discuss this chapter in detail in my chapter 3 on "Yin & Yang, Qi, Dao & De."
4. I will discuss this chapter in detail in chapter 3 below.

2 The Dao of Sex

1. The Mawangdui and many other versions mention literally the "penis" (*zui*) in this chapter (ch.55). In the Wang Bi version we instead find the word *whole* (*quan*) which does not really make sense.

Yin and Yang, Qi, Dao and De

1. Marcel Granet, *La pensée chinoise* (Paris: Éditions Albin Michel, 1934), 108.
2. Granet, *Pensée*, 269.
3. *Dazhuan* (or, *Xici*), sec. 2.
4. Granet, *Pensée*, 269.
5. Following Julian Jaynes, the same was the case in ancient Greece: "The Aristotelian writings, for example, located consciousness or the abode of thought in and just above the heart, believing the brain to be a mere cooling organ since it was insensitive to touch or injury." Jaynes, *The Origin of Consciousness in the Breakdown of the Bicameral Mind* (Boston: Houghton Mifflin, 1976), 44.
6. When the *Laozi* speaks about the sage ruler, I am using the male pronoun for historical reasons. It would be an anachronism to assume that the *Laozi* was referring to both sexes when it comes to rulers. Rulers in ancient China were normally men.
7. Cf. Herbert Fingarette, *Confucius: The Secular as Sacred* (New York: Harper Torchbooks), 1972.
8. Roger T. Ames and David Hall, *Daodejing: "Making This Life Significant": A Philosophical Translation* (New York: Ballantine, 2003), 65. See also an earlier version of this definition in Roger T. Ames and Henry Rosemont, *The Analects of Confucius: A Philosophical Translation* (New York: Ballantine, 1998), 47.
9. Cf. Ames and Hall, *Daodejing*, 228.
10. Niklas Luhmann, *Einführung in die Systemtheorie* (Heidelberg: Carl-Auer-Sysme, 2002), 110–111 (my translation).

Paradox Politics

1. For such a reconstruction of the Mawangdui manuscripts of the *Laozi*, see Michael Friedrich, "Zur Datierung zweier Handschriften des *Daode jing*," *Text-Kritische Beiträge* 2 (1996): 105–117.
2. See J. J. Clarke, *The Tao of the West: Western Transformations of Taoist Thought* (London: Routledge, 2000), 84.

On War

1. On von Clausewitz and Chinese philosophy, see François Jullien, *A Treatise on Efficacy: Between Western and Chinese Thinking* (Honolulu: University of Hawai'i Press, 2004).
2. I use the male pronoun again for historical reasons. Military leaders in ancient China were usually men.

NOTES   155

3. See Robert G. Henricks, *Lao-Tzu. Te-Tao Ching: A New Translation Based on the Recently Discovered Ma-Wang-Tui Texts* (New York: Ballantine, 1989), 164.

4. Roger T. Ames and David Hall, *Daodejing: "Making This Life Significant": A Philosophical Translation* (New York: Ballantine, 2003), 185.

5. *Zuozhuan*, Duke Zhuang, tenth year.

6. Günter Wohlfart, *Die Kunst des Lebens und andere Künste: Skurrile Skizzen zu einem eurodaoistischen Ethos ohne Moral* (forthcoming).

6 Masters of Satisfaction (Desires, Emotions, and Addictions)

1. In this passage, as is often the case, filial piety toward one's parents is mentioned along with the "fraternal love" (*di*) to one's (elder) brother. These two are, from a Confucian point of view, the main components of the proper emotional and behavioral development of a child, and thus consequentially, for the development of a harmonious society undisturbed by social unrest and selfish attempts to usurp personal power. Here is the complete passage as translated by Ames and Rosemont: "Master You said: 'It is a rare thing for someone who has a sense of filial and fraternal responsibility (*xiao di*) to have a taste for defying authority. And it is unheard of for those who have no taste for defying authority to be keen on initiating rebellion. Exemplary persons (*junzi*) concentrate their efforts on the root, for the root having taken hold, the way (*dao*) will grow therefrom. As for filial and fraternal responsibility, it is, I suspect, the root of authoritative conduct (*ren*)." (Roger T. Ames and Henry Rosemont, *The Analects of Confucius: A Philosophical Translation* [New York: Ballantine, 1998], 71.) Accordingly, "rebels," from a Confucian perspective, were people who, because of a lack of emotional attachments, strive to overthrow established social structures and governments, i.e., their political "family" and "parents," for reasons of personal gain.

2. Niklas Luhmann, *The Reality of the Mass Media* (Stanford: Stanford University Press, 2000), 21.

7 Indifference and Negative Ethics

1. Quoted from Lin Yutang, *Translations from the Chinese (The Importance of Understanding)* (Cleveland: Forum Books, World Publishing, 1963), 385. Lin's rendition is not an exact translation. The original text can be found in *Huainanzi, Zhuzi jicheng* edition (Beijing: Zhonghua, 1954), 310–11. I modified Lin Yutang's rendering of the last sentence and translated it more literally to highlight its linguistic parallelism to chapter 58 from the *Laozi*, quoted below.

2. In translating *xing* as "disposition," I follow James Behuniak Jr., *Mencius on Becoming Human* (Albany: State University of New York Press, 2005). I have proposed

such a reading in my article "Menschenrechte, Missionare, Menzius. Überlegungen angesichts der Frage nach der Kompatibilität von Konfuzianismus und Menschenrechten," in Günter Schubert, ed., *Menschenrechte in Ostasien* (Tübingen: Mohr und Siebeck, 1999), 109–122.

3. *Mencius* 2A.6, quoted from the translation by D. C. Lau, *Mencius* (London: Penguin Books, 1970), 82–83.

4. See also the chapters on "Ethics" and "Daoism and Contemporary Philosophy" in my book *Daoism Explained: From the Dream of the Butterfly to the Fishnet Allegory* (Chicago: Open Court, 2004), as well as my article "Moral und Pathologie: Niklas Luhmann, die Massenmedien und der Daoismus," in Rolf Elberfeld, ed., *Komparative Ethik: Das gute Leben zwischen den Kulturen* (Cologne: Edition Chora, 2002), 303–18.

Permanence and Eternity

1. I am exclusively referring here to Augustine's philosophy of time in the *Confessions*, and not to the quite different concept presented in the *City of God*.

2. John K. Ryan (trans.), *The Confessions of Augustine* (Garden City, N.Y.: Image Books, 1960), 282. Subsequent quotations from this edition are cited in the text.

Death and the Death Penalty

1. See the chapter on death in my book *Daoism Explained: From the Dream of the Butterfly to the Fishnet Allegory* (Chicago: Open Court, 2004).

2. In the Mawangdui manuscripts, this sentence says in a more Confucian tone: "To die, but not to *be forgotten*—this is longevity" (emphasis added). The Chinese words and characters for "to perish" (*wang*) and "to be forgotten" (*wang*) are similar.

3. In order to understand the role of the death penalty in the ancient Chinese penal system, it should be mentioned that imprisonment was seldom practiced. "Milder" penalties than capital punishment included bodily mutilations and other bodily punishments. Capital punishment itself was gradually differentiated into more and less cruel and painful types of execution.

4. I follow here the interpretation and translation of my German edition of the text *Laotse: Tao Te King* (Frankfurt am Main: Fischer, 1995), 131–32. Most other commentators and translators (both Chinese and Western) read this passage in a different way and take it to be a statement against the death penalty in general. I believe it to be a statement *against the execution* but *not against the institution* of the death penalty. (As explained here, I believe that according to the paradoxical Daoist way of argumentation, the *Laozi*'s view of the death penalty is that it should "act without acting.") I believe my interpretation to be in line with the context of the *Laozi* that insists (as

in the above-mentioned chapters) on the importance of the fear of (premature) death among the people and also to be in accordance with the philological evidence from the Mawangdui manuscripts, which here explicitly speak of the "death penalty" as opposed to the later standard text edition that most other commentaries and interpretations are based on. An overview of the majority interpretation as well as a reference to the minority interpretation that I concur with is found in Huang Zhao, *Boshu Laozi jiaozhu xi* (Analysis and collated commentaries on the silk manuscripts of the *Laozi*) (Taibei: Xuesheng shuju, 1991), 399.

5. Friedrich Nietzsche, *Götzen-Dämmerung* (*Twilight of the Idols*), "Die vier grossen Irrthümer" ("The four great errors"), in Giorgio Colli and Mazzino Montinari, eds., *Sämtliche Werke: Kritische Studienausgabe*, vol. 6 (Munich: DTV, 1980), 95–96. Nietzsche's verdict of Christianity as a "metaphysics of the hangman" is reaffirmed by the contemporary German philosopher Peter Sloterdijk. Sloterdijk highlights the interconnectedness between Christian free will and human guilt and writes: "Man's overburdening with guilt as it is condensed in the concept of original sin is an effect of an increasing reliance on arguments from freedom for explaining the motivation of evil within the total reality created by God." Peter Sloterdijk, *Nicht gerettet: Versuche nach Heidegger* (Frankfurt am Main: Suhrkamp, 2001), 92.

6. The central role of the individualization and personalization within the Western philosophy of the death penalty goes back to the philosophy of Immanuel Kant. Kant argues in *The Metaphysics of Morals* (see the English translation by Mary Gregor, *The Metaphysics of Morals* [Cambridge: Cambridge University Press, 1991], 140–45) that any wrongdoing can be ascribed to the "inner wickedness" (*innere Bösartigkeit*) of the innate personality of the offender. Unlike natural punishment, punishment by a court recognizes the criminal as a person or as a free individual. Kant views this recognition—and here he is surely in line with a Christian metaphysics of the hangman—as being at the core of justice, which he fittingly describes in its punitive dimension as the "law of retribution" (*ius talionis, Wiedervergeltungsrecht*). Kant derides a primitive pre-Christian philosophy of the death penalty, which is not founded on retribution but (as in Daoism) on deterrence. He calls the maxim of deterrence "It is better for one man to die than for an entire people to perish" a "Pharisaical saying" and thinks that with it justice vanishes. A death penalty based on Kantian justice is based on principle and reason and not on sheer practical or natural purposes, as Kant illustrates with the following example: "if a people inhabiting an island decided to separate and disperse throughout the world, the last murderer remaining in prison would first have to be executed, so that each has done to him what his deeds deserve." The death penalty is a "metaphysical" duty that cannot be neglected, even if it makes no practical sense. It is, so to speak, a necessary moral cleansing. Even if it is of no use, the Kantian hangman has to hang for the sake of Kantian metaphysics.

Interestingly enough, the Kantian metaphysics of the death penalty, based on the "inner personality," considers the death penalty dubious when it comes to "crimes of honor." Kant gives the following example: Killing "a child that comes into the world apart from marriage" should be considered an action arising from a sense of honor. In this case, capital punishment is not to be sought since, on the one hand, the killing was done in defense of personal honor and, on the other hand, the victim lacked a personality. This is, according to Kant, due to the fact that an illegitimate child had "stolen into the commonwealth (like contraband merchandise), so that the commonwealth can ignore its existence (since it rightly should not have come to exist in this way), and can therefore also ignore its annihilation." Since in this case the offender has no "inner wickedness" and the killed child—being "illegitimate" and thus lacking the status of personhood—does not qualify as a victim, retribution is out of place and the death penalty inappropriate.

Contemporary American death penalty philosophy is the immediate heir of this specific Christian-Kantian philosophy of the "inner wickedness" of offenders and the retribution of "innocent victims." It insists on the freedom of the individual in order to declare the person guilty, and the more freedom, the more guilt. Peter Sloterdijk observes: "It cannot be a coincidence that the penal system of the United States is the most extensive and most intensive of the world and that in proportion to the population the number of inmates in American prisons is nearly ten times higher than in Europe—and it continues to grow" (Sloterdijk, *Nicht gerettet*, 121).

In a very Kantian manner, the American author Herbert Morris states: "A man has the right to be punished rather than treated [therapeutically, H.G.M.] if he is guilty of some offense" (Morris, "Person and Punishment," in Robert M. Baird and Stuart E. Rosenbaum, eds., *Philosophy of Punishment* [Buffalo: Prometheus Books, 1988], 67–82; 78). The recognition of the offender's free personality brings about his guilt and punishment. Walter Berns, another American author, stresses this point when he speaks of a "morality of anger." The evil wrongdoer becomes the object of a just indignation of the other free beings around him. Punishment is thus understood as an expression of moral anger and as a kind of social catharsis. According to Berns, "there is something in the souls of men ... that requires ... crimes to be revenged" ("The Morality of Anger," in Baird and Rosenbaum, eds., *Philosophy of Punishment*, 85–93; 89). Even though there is, at least to my knowledge, no psychological evidence of this asserted universal characteristic of the "souls of men," the American penal system recognizes and encourages the supposed need and right for the revenge of the victims of a crime—for instance, by reserving seats for victims and their family at an execution. Revenge, dignity, and the cult of the victim are closely related elements of the semantics of the free individual. Justice is supposed to inspire reverence for the free human being. And the American nation inspires such reverence among its citizens, at least according to Berns, by not abolishing the death penalty. By insisting on the death penalty, Berns argues, the United States "will remind its citizens that it is a country worthy of heroes" (93). Heroism, respect for the individual, morality, indignation, and the revenge of the victim are inseparable. Berns declares: "We punish criminals principally in order to pay them back, and we execute the worst of them out of *moral necessity*" (85; emphasis added). The American philosophy of the death penalty, which advocates the heroic and metaphysical killings on moral principle, culminates in the works of Ernest van den Haag. Van den Haag not only reflects on a Christian-Kantian duty to hang, he also reflects on the necessity for reasonably tough and immediate executions. In regard to the Kantian notion of the law of retribution, van den Haag goes even further. Deserved punishment, he thinks, must be undeservedly tough because "the offender imposed undeserved suffering on his victim. Why should society not impose undeserved ... suffering on the offender?" (van den Haag, "Refuting Reiman and Nathanson," in Baird and Rosenbaum, eds., *Philosophy of Punishment*, 141–51; 142). Kant already pointed out that penal law primarily aims at "inflicting pain" on the criminal (*The Metaphysics of Morals*, 140). According to van den Haag, this pain must be very intense. An offender, by violating the law, not only makes a victim suffer but also society as a whole. "Hence," van den Haag says, "punishment must, whenever possible, impose pain believed to exceed the pain suffered by the individual victim of the crime. No less is deserved" (van den Haag, *ibid.*, 143).

10 "*Without the Impulses of Man*": A Daoist Critique of Humanism

1. I am quoting A. C. Graham's translation with slight modifications: A. C. Graham, *Chuang Tzu: The Inner Chapters* (Indianapolis and Cambridge: Hackett, 2001), 82. For the original, see the *Zhuzi jicheng* edition of the *Zhuangzi jishi* (Peking: Zhonghua: 1954), 99–100.

2. Graham translates *qing* here somewhat unconventionally as "essentials." (See previous note.)

3. There is an alternative reading of this passage which interprets the last two characters not as meaning "straw dogs," but as "straw *and* dogs." This interpretation goes back to Wang Bi's commentary. I, however, follow the reading of Wing-tsit Chan, *The Way of Lao Tzu* (Indianapolis: Bobbs-Merrill, 1963), 107, and many others. The following analysis follows in part my article, "The Discarding of Straw Dogs (Thinking Through the *Laozi*)," in Ewing Chinn and Henry Rosemont Jr., eds., *Metaphilosophy and Chinese Thought: Interpreting David Hall* (New York: Global Scholarly Publications: 2005).

4. Chen Guying gives an overview of commentaries in *Laozi zhu yi ji pingjie* (Peking: Xinhua, 1984), 78–84. This book has been translated by R.Y. W. Young and

Roger T. Ames: *Lao Tzu: Text, Notes, and Comments* (San Francisco: Chinese Materials Center. 1981).

5. Graham, *Chuang Tzu*, 192.

6. Ibid., 88.

7. Roger T. Ames and David Hall, *Daodejing:"Making This Life Significant": A Philosophical Translation* (New York: Ballantine, 2003).

8. Michel Foucault, *The Order of Things: An Archaeology of the Human Sciences* (New York: Vintage, 1994), 386–87.

9. See the series of articles on "automaticity" in *American Psychologist* 54.7 (July 1999).

INDEX

abstinence, sexual, 25
acting through non-action (*wei wu wei*):
    in death penalty, 128, 156*n*4 (ch.9);
    in Qi exercise, 38; by sage-rulers, 25,
    59–61, 143
addiction: desire for knowledge as,
    95–97; prevention of, 94
Ames, Roger T., 81, 138
Analects, Confucian: on filial piety,
    88–89; *Laozi* compared with, 3
anger: morality of, 158*n*6
anti-activism, Daoist, 77–78
Aristotle: on creation, 52
astronomy: function of, 113
attitude, judgmental, 134–35
Augustine (Saint): on time vs. eternity,
    118–20, 156*n*1 (ch.8)
autopoiesis, 50–51

bad luck, 99–102
barrenness: fertility and, 69–70
beginning of time, 115–17

bellows: as structured image, 10
Berns, Walter, 158*n*6
Book of Changes: oracular formulae of,
    102; twoness in, 34; Yin/Yang as
    complementary moments in, 35

calendar: function of, 113–14
calmness: cultivation of, 97
capitalist economy: as general addiction, 94
capital punishment, 126–30; abuse of,
    128–29; acting through non-action,
    128, 156*n*4 (ch.9); age restrictions on,
    127; American philosophy of, 158*n*6–
    159*n*6; in Chinese penal system,
    126–27, 156*n*3 (ch.9); for crimes of
    honor, 158*n*6; as deterrent, 127–30,
    157*n*6; Kant on, 157*n*6–159*n*6; Western, as metaphysics of the hangman,
    129–30, 157*n*5, 157*n*6–158*n*6; Western
    views of, 128–30
cessation, mastery of, 114–15

change: acceptance of, 99–101, 111; complementary (opposite) segments of, 102–104; cycle of, 100–101; phases of, 103; philosophy of, 102
Chinese philosophy: divination in, 102; Mencius on, x
Christianity: conception of time, 118–20; God as creator in, 52; humanism of, 140–42; immortal soul in, 125–26; metaphysics of the hangman in, 129–30, 157*n*5, 157*n*6–158*n*6
ci, 26
communication: changing nature of, 142–43
concentration: of Qi, 37–38
Confessions of Augustine, 118–20
Confucianism: *Analects* vs. *Laozi*, 3; behaviorism in, 89; filial piety in, 88–89, 155*n*1 (ch.6); moral virtues in, 107–108; obsession with death, 136; ritualism of, 136–37
consciousness: heart as center of, 38, 154*n*5
consumption, 91
Copernicus, 145
cosmic processes: creation of, 51; gender in, 26; humans in, 49, 70–71, 138–140; procreation in, 138–39
cosmology: of *Laozi*, 50–52
creation: models of, 51–53
crimes of honor, 158*n*6

Daodejing (*Laozi*): as assembly of images, 19–29; authorship of, 3, 138; cultural context of, 1–3; darkness of, 1, 7; English translations of, 149–52; how to read, 1–20; as hypertext, 5–7, 142; as leadership text, 56, 57; as manual for immortality, 121–22; nonhumanist characteristics of, 137–38; oral nature of, 1–2, 4; rhetorical linkages in, 6–13, 20; structural characteristics of, 3–4, 142, 143; textual history of, 147–48
Daoism: attitudes toward time, 119–20; critique of humanism, 133–45; Dao of heaven (*tian*), 45–47, 48; efficacy in, 20, 41–43; femininity and masculinity in, 26; humans as part of larger order in, 55–57; as integrated order of cosmos, 48; oneness in, 40–41; revolving around empty center, 56; unity of, 40–41; as way of living and dying, 21; Yin/Yang as rhythm of, 35–36
dark (*xuan*), 16
darkness: as female quality, 16–17; fertility and, 69–70; of *Laozi*, 1, 7
Darwin, Charles, 145
De: as efficacy of Dao, 20, 41–43
death, 121–31; avoidance of, 121; Confucian obsession with, 136; European philosophies of, 125–26; fear of, 125–26; interdependence with life, 122–23, 125; prevention of, 124 (*see also* immortality); untimely, 126
death penalty. *See* capital punishment
Deleuze, Gilles, 141–42
demiurge: creation and, 52
democracy: groups excluded from, 73; paradox politics of *Laozi* vs., 71–72
deterrence: capital punishment as, 129–30, 157*n*6
disasters, natural: as interrupted cycles, 112–13
disorder (*luan*) vs. order (*zhi*), x. *See also* social disorder

INDEX

economy: capitalist, as general addiction, 94; lack of human agency in, 144; market, *Laozi* not addressing, 91
efficacy: of Dao, 20, 41–43; images of, 11–12; sage-ruler as source of, 57–59; of valley, 12–13
ego, 145
emotions: in Confucianism, 88–89; creating social disorder, 96–97; as judgmental attitude, 134–35; knowledge claims and, 101. *See also* human desires
energy: Qi as, 36–37
environment: humanist politics and, 72–73
equanimity, 100–101
eroticism: absence in *Laozi*, 29–30; Greek philosophers on, 30–32
Eryximachos: on Eros, 30, 31
eternity: time vs., 118–20. *See also* permanence
executions. *See* capital punishment

family: as core social unit, 88–89, 155*n*1 (ch.6)
fasting, emotional, 89
femininity: Dao concept of, 26; darkness as quality of, 16–17; female sexuality and, 22–23; structure of, 15–16; water and, 14–15, 23; Yin as, 33, 34
Fengshui: cycle of life and, 26–27
fertility: darkness and barrenness as sources of, 69–70; Platonic love and, 31; as primary sexual characteristic, 23; river and, 21; united duality of, 21–22, 27–28; of valley, 9–11, 28; world as cycle of, 33

filial piety: of Confucianism, 88–89, 155*n*1 (ch.6)
flow: imagery of, 41
Foucault, Michel, 141–42
fraternal love, 155*n*1 (ch.6)
free will, 130, 144–45, 157*n*5
Freud, Sigmund, 144–45
funeral rites, 89

gate: image of, 17
gender, 26
God: as creator, 52
good luck, 100–102
Graham, A. C., 56
Granet, Marcel, 34–36
Gray, John, 153*n*4 (ch.1)
Greek philosophy: creation models in, 52–53; sexuality in, 30–32
guilt, 130, 157*n*5
Guodian texts, 1
Guo Xiang, 122

Hall, David, 81, 138
Han dynasty, 147
hangman, 128; metaphysics of, 129–30, 157*n*5, 157*n*6–158*n*6
harmony: creative, 35; social, 76–77
heart: as center of consciousness, 38, 154*n*5
heaven (*tian*): Chinese concept of, 44–45; Dao of, 45–47, 48; mandate of, for sage-rulers, 65–66; as natural order, 17
heaven and earth (*tian di*): process between, 47–48, 113; sage-ruler as representative of, 73, 135–36; society following rhythms of, 138; ten thousand things in, 34

hedonism, paradoxical, 94
Hemingway, Ernest, 83
Henricks, Robert G.., 81
heroism: heroes as moral agents, 84; Western vs. Daoist views of, 82–83
Huainanzi, 99, 101
human agency, 143–45
human behavior: Confucians on, 89; order vs. disorder in, 56–57
human character: four germs of, 108–109; judgmental attitudes in, 134–35; sages untouched by, 133–36
human desires, 87–97; as addiction, 94–95; causing social disorder, 87; for knowledge, 95–97; minimizing, for social harmony, 76–77; paradox of fulfilling, 91–93; politics of, 90–91; sensual, optimizing, 93–94; as state of discontent, 94. *See also* emotions
humanism: Christian model of, 140–42; Daoist critique of, 133–45; dehumanization of humane in, 139; human agency in, 143–45; immanence of humankind and, 139–40; interdependence of human and cosmic processes, 138–39; paradox politics of *Laozi* vs., 71–74; ritualism of, 136–37; semantics of, 140–41; war and, 85–86
human life: Daoist vs. Western views of, 55–57; following rhythm of heaven and earth, 138
human society: in cosmic processes, 49, 70–71, 138–39; self-so mechanisms of, 48–49. *See also* social disorder; social systems
hundun (undifferentiated), 29

hygiene, 126
hypertext: of Internet, 4–5; *Laozi* as, 5–7, 142

ideal man: as infant, 24
images: of efficacy, 11–12; flow in, 41; gate in, 17; *Laozi* as assembly of, 19–20; negative shapes in, 9–11; of productivity, 13; of roots, 17–19, 89–90; sexual, 29, 35; structured, 8, 10; of uncarved wood, 8–9; valley in, 7–9, 28; as visualization of strategies, 8; of water, 8–9, 13–14
immanence of humankind, 139–40
immortality: *Laozi* as manual for achieving, 121–22; loss of individuality and, 125; of soul, 125–26; valley spirit as, 7
impulse, natural: morality vs., 109–110
indifference: acceptance of change as, 100–101, 111; in moral evaluations, 105–107; of sage-rulers, 136–37
individuality: immortality and loss of, 125
infant: idealized man as, 24; male sexuality of, 24–25; presexuality of, 29; relation to valley and river, 28
information society: as addiction, 95–96
instant, presence of, 120
interaction: social, opposites in, 105; Yin/Yang rubrics of, 35
intercourse, sexual, 22–24. *See also* sexuality
Internet: communication on, 142; hypertext of, 4–5

Jaynes, Julian, 154n5
Judaism: on God as creator, 52

INDEX

Kant, Immanuel, 157n6–159n6
knowledge: claims, minimization of, 101; creating social disorder, 96–97; desire for, as addiction, 95–97

language: opposites in, 105
Laozi. See Daodejing (Laozi)
leadership: Laozi as text for, 56, 57. See also military leader; sage-rulers
"lethal weapon" warrior, 83
Lévi-Strauss, Claude, 35
life: cycle of, 26–27; human, 55–57, 138; interdependence with death, 122–23, 125
Lin Yutang, 99
literary analysis: of Laozi, 143
longevity (shou), 156n2 (ch.9); as process, 122; right time for dying and, 123–24; social/natural, 125
luck: alteration of good and bad, 99, 102; as change process, 99–102
Luhmann, Niklas, 50–51, 95

male sexuality: of infant, 24–25; masculinity and, 26, 33, 34; as movement and stiffness, 23; Platonic, 31; retention of semen in, 22
man, concept of: as European invention, 141
market economy, 91, 144
martial arts, 80
masculinity: Dao concept of, 26; Yang as, 33, 34
mastery of cessation (zhi zhi), 114–15
Maturna, Humberto, 50–51
meaning: Laozi as source of, 2
medical practices, 126
medium (energy): Qi as, 36–37
Mencius, x, 108–109

The Metaphysics of Morals (Kant), 157n6–159n6
military leader: as antihero, 83–84; gender of, 154n2 (ch.5); political ruler as, 76
morality and moral distinctions: of anger, 158n6; in Confucianism, 107–108; indifference of sage to, 105–107; natural impulse vs., 109–110; as social pathology, 110; volatility of, 106; war and, 84
movement: in sexual intercourse, 22
mu, 26
muddy water: image of, 8–9
multiplicity: world of, 40

Napoleon, 82
nationalism: in warfare, 84–85
natural impulse: morality vs., 109–110
natural order, 33; heaven as, 17; human culture and, 139; interruption of productivity in, 112–13; permanence of processes in, 111–12
negative shapes: images of, 9–11
Nietzsche, Friedrich, 129–30, 141, 144
non-action (wu wei), 59–61, 143. See also acting through non-action (wei wu wei)
non-agency principle, 74, 143
non-presence: of sage-rulers, 58; vs. presence, 34, 39
numbers: as symbols, 12

old age. See longevity (shou)
"old man at the fort" (story), 99–101
oneness, 40–41
ongoing, as natural process, 18–19
opposites: in change, 102–104; in social interaction, 105

The Order of Things (Foucault), 141
order (*zhi*): Dao of heaven and, 45–46, 48; disorder (*luan*) vs., x
overcast sky (*yin-tian*), 35

paradox: of fulfilling desires, 91–93; of politics, 55–74 (*see also* politics); in totalitarianism, 71–72; in warfare strategies, 79–82
passivity: of sage-rulers, 25; as war strategy, 79–82
Patton, George S., 83
penal system, Chinese, 126–27, 156n3 (ch.9)
permanence, 111–20; eternity vs., 119; mastery of cessation in, 114–15; of natural processes, 111–12; as perfect form of time, 115; structure of, 117
philosophy: of change, 102; Chinese, x, 102; Greek, sexuality in, 30–32; post-humanist, 141–42, 144–45; of time, 111
pin, 26
Platonic eroticism, 30–31, 32
politics: archaic nature of, in *Laozi*, 71–72; bias-free participants in, 73–74; central position of ruler in, 57–59, 71; dehumanization of, 75–76; of desire, 90–91; distinction between ruler and ruled in, 57–59, 68–69; lack of human agency in, 143–44; non-action of ruler in, 59–61; non-agency principle in, 74, 143; paradox of, 55–74; political ruler as military leader, 76; present-day, from *Laozi* perspective, 72–74; in regulation of human interests, 73; as sign of decay in society, 62; as source of problems, 75; war as failure of, 75–76. *See also* sage-rulers
position, sexual, 22
post-humanist philosophy, 141–42, 144–45
presence: of instant in time, 120; vs. non-presence, 34, 39
presexual, the, 29
procreation: as cosmic process, 138–39; duality of, 22; giving and taking in, 27–28; permanence cycles in, 111–12
productivity: images of, 13

Qi: acting through non-action in exercise, 38; concentration of, 37–38; as medium (energy), 36–37; Yin/Yang as aspects of, 37, 38–39
Qi Gong: techniques of, 37
Qin dynasty: Legalist tyranny of, 72
qing (feeling; emotion), 134

reproduction. *See* procreation
rhizome, 141
ritualism, Confucian, 136–37
river, 21, 28
root: in Confucianism, 88–89; image of, Daoist, 17–19, 89–90
rubrics: of Yin/Yang, 34–35

sage-rulers: absence of self-esteem and success of, 63–64; administration of time by, 113–14; allowing natural course of events, 48–49; central position of, 57–59, 87; characteristics of, 59; gender of, 154n6; lack of political ambition of, 62–63, 87–88, 90, 102–104; mandate of heaven of, 65–66; neutrality of, 64–65;

INDEX

non-action of, 25, 59–61, 143; noninterference with self-so, 139; nonpresence of, 57–59, 67–70; ordering of twoness by, 43; political goal of, 76; remoteness from humanity of, 133–37; as representative of heaven and earth, 73, 135–36; self-designations of, 70; self-restraint of, 77; sexual abstinence of, 25; as source of efficacy, 57–59; as uniter of social functions, 70–71
seasons, 111–13
self-generation: autopoiesis and, 51
self-so (*ziran*): as creation model, 52–53; in evolution of *Laozi* text, 138; in mechanisms of society, 48–49; noninterference by sages with, 61, 139
semen: retention of, 22
sexuality, 21–32; as cosmic process, 138; female, 22–23 (*see also* femininity); in Greek philosophy, 30–32; human vs. non-human, 26–27; intercourse and, 22–24; latency of, 32; male (*see* male sexuality); of male infant, 24–25; masculine and feminine vs. gender, 26; non-anthophomorphic, 26–27; non-erotic, in *Laozi*, 29–30; non-sexuality of Daoist sage, 25; presexual in, 28–29; sensual desires and, 93–94; as struggle between partners, 22–23; united duality of, 21–22, 27–28, 33; Yin/Yang imagery of, 35
sheng (life). *See* life
shou. *See* longevity (*shou*)
Sloterdijk, Peter, 157n5, 158n6
social disorder: desires causing, 87; knowledge creating, 96–97; morality as, 110

social systems: autopoiesis in, 50–51; ruler's role as uniter of, 70–71
Socrates: on Eros, 30–32
soul: concept of, 120; immortality of, 125–26
stillness: in sexual intercourse, 22
strategy: image as visualization of, 8; of reversal, 59
Straw Dogs: Thoughts on Humans and Other Animals (Gray), 153n4 (ch.1)
straw dogs (*chu gou*), 135–37, 159n3
sun (*tai-yang*), 35
Sunzi tradition, 81
symbols: numbers as, 12

tai-yang (sun), 35
threeness, 40
tian. *See* heaven (*tian*)
tian-xia (under heaven), 45
time: beginning of, 115–17; correct administration of, 113–14; Daoist vs. Christian attitudes toward, 119–20; heavenly vs. human, 113; "mother" of, 116; permanence as perfect form of, 115; philosophy of, 111; presence of instant in, 120; rhythmic, 111–12; St. Augustine on, 118–20, 156n1 (ch.8)
timeliness, 113–15
tools: sexual imagery of, 29
totalitarianism: paradox politics as, 71–72
truth, eternal, 118
twoness, 33–34, 40

uncarved wood: image of, 8–9; presexual nature of, 28–29; sage-rulers as, 66

under heaven (*tian-xia*), 45
undifferentiated (*hundun*), 29

valley: efficacy of, 12–13; fertility of, 9–11, 28; image of, 7–9, 28; linkage with water, 13–14, 28; quality of, 8
van den Haag, Ernest, 159*n*6
vanity, human, 144–45
Varela, Francisco, 50–51
von Clausewitz, Carl, 75, 84

Wang Bi, 148
warfare, 75–86; art of, 80; as failure of politics, 75–76; heroism in, 82–84; human desires causing, 76–77; humanist vs. nonhumanist ideologies in, 85–86; *Laozi* contempt for, 78; moral dimensions of, 84; nationalism in, 84–85; paradoxical strategies for, 79–82; political ruler as military leader in, 76; as social disaster, 84–85; *Sunzi* tradition of, 81; weapons in, 77–79; Western traditions vs. Daoist nonengagement, 82–86
Warring States (*zhan guo*), 56, 76
warriors, 82–83, 84
water: feminine and, 14–15, 23; imagery of, 8–9, 13–14; linkage with valley, 13–14, 28

weapons, 77–79
weather, 27
wei wu wei. *See* acting through non-action (*wei wu wei*)
Wohlfart, Günter, 82
world, 45
writing, Chinese, 2
wu (non-presence): of sage-rulers, 58; vs. presence (*you*), 34, 39
wu wei (non-action), 59–61, 143

xiong, 26
xuan (dark), 16

yin-tian (overcast sky), 35
Yin/Yang: as aspects of Qi, 37, 38–39; in *Laozi*, 34; as rhythmic structure of cosmos, 35–36; rubrics of, 34–35; twoness of, 33–34
you (presence), 34, 39

zhan guo (Warring States), 56, 76
zhi (order): Dao of heaven and, 45–46, 48; disorder (*luan*) vs., x
zhi zhi (mastery of cessation), 114–15
Zhuangzi, 122, 133–34, 135
ziran. *See* self-so (*ziran*)
Zuozhuan, 81

GPSR Authorized Representative: Easy Access System Europe, Mustamäe tee 50, 10621 Tallinn, Estonia, gpsr.requests@easproject.com

www.ingramcontent.com/pod-product-compliance
Lightning Source LLC
Chambersburg PA
CBHW070831300426
44111CB00014B/2520